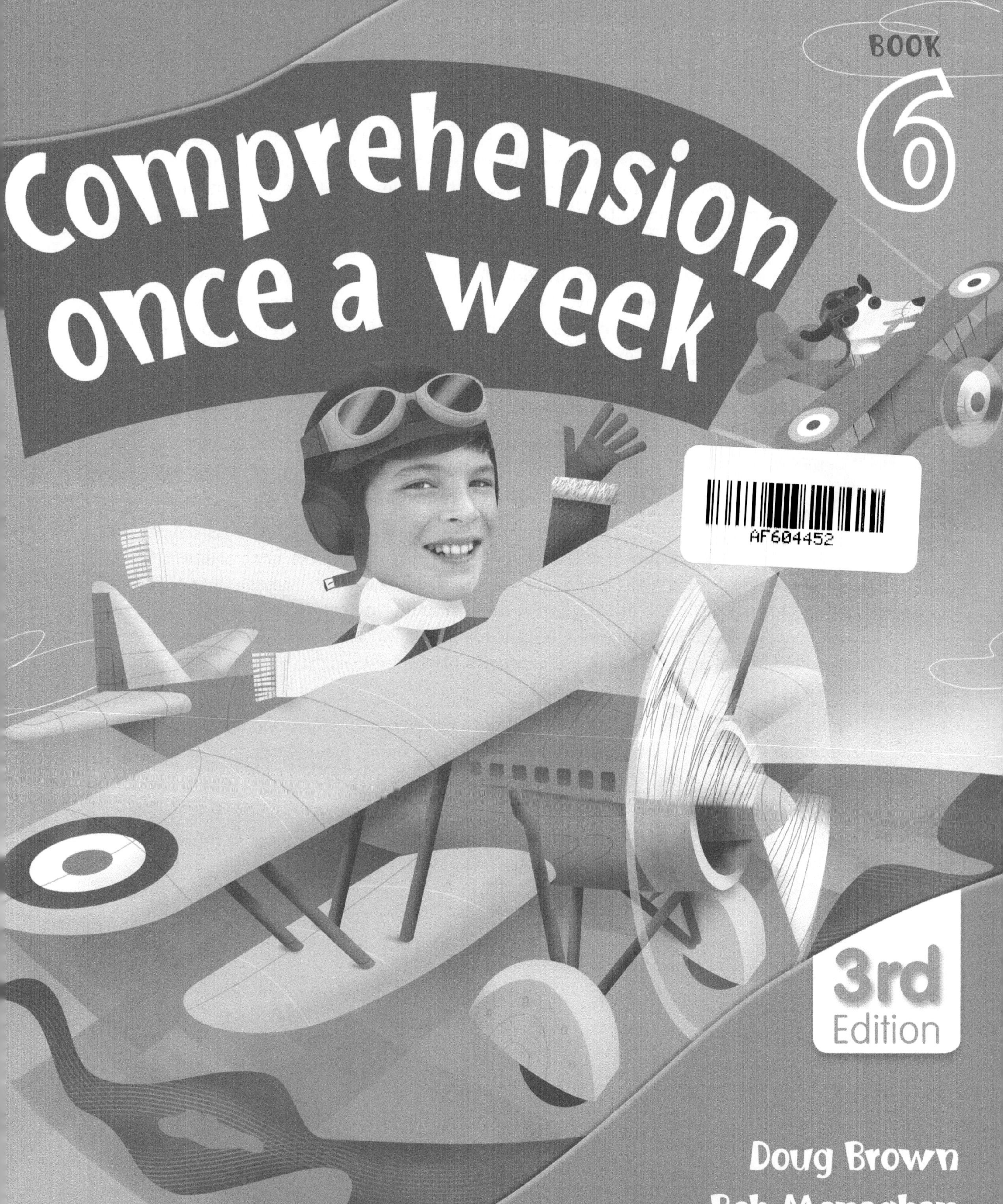
BOOK
6
Comprehension once a week
AF604452
3rd
Edition
Doug Brown
Bob Monaghan

Introduction

Comprehension Once a Week is a series of six graded student activity books. Through a variety of text types and comprehension focuses the series aims to develop and improve children's comprehension skills, to assist them in making sense of real-life materials they might encounter in daily life.

The wide spectrum of reading texts includes factual and fictional accounts, newspaper reports, diary entries, reports, travel brochures, songs, literature and calendars. These are explored as examples of recounts, procedural texts, information reports/factual descriptions, explanations, expositions, narratives and poetic texts. This variety will alert children to the versatility of literature and its importance in their lives. Teachers are encouraged to provide samples of other text types.

By blending interesting and humorous content, the children will be keen to read the text and engage in the related activities. Both literal and inferential comprehension skills are practised. Clear critical thinking and problem solving are encouraged throughout the series.

Each of Books 3 to 6 consists of 35 double-page units (one per week), each comprising a stimulus page and an activity page. Extension exercises entitled 'Moving on' are provided at the conclusion of each unit to allow students to further explore their reading experiences. It is suggested that the books be used sequentially as the units are graded in difficulty. However, units can also be chosen to suit a relevant topic being studied in the classroom.

Generally, Book 1 is aimed at children in their second year of school and Book 6 at students in their final primary school year. This is, of course, flexible to suit the standard and needs of the students.

A skills overview is provided at the beginning of each book. In addition, the text type is indicated at the foot of each stimulus page and the comprehension focus at the foot of each activity page. Answers are provided in a removable insert in the middle of Books 3 to 6.

Doug Brown

Bob Monaghan

Elske Brown

Danah Tiltman

Contents

Skills Overview

Week	Title	Text Type	Comprehension Focus
1	Now for the Bad News	Narrative – Comic Strip	Literal and Inferential Questioning
2	A Fable	Narrative – Fable	Literal Questioning
3	Famous Headlines	Information – Headlines	Matching Headlines to Newspaper Reports / Inferential / Questioning
4	Ham and Pineapple Pizza	Procedural – Recipe	Literal Questioning
5	Weird and Wonderful	Information – Factual Description	Completing a Crossword / Recalling Detail
6	Up, Up and Away	Information – Timeline	True or False / Recalling Detail
7	Top 20	Information – Lists	Literal Questioning
8	Happy Harry's Hamburger Heaven	Exposition – Menu	Cloze Activity
9	How to Eat a Meat Pie	Procedural – Instructions	Ordering Sequence of Events / Answering 'Why' Questions
10	The Wild Colonial Boy	Narrative – Song	Finding Answers in a Wordsearch / Recalling Detail
11	Big	Information – Factual Description	Matching / Recalling Detail
12	The Magic Jar	Narrative – Traditional Tale	Multiple-choice Cloze Activity
13	Children's Week	Exposition – Program	Literal Questioning / Ordering Sequence of Events
14	For Sale	Exposition – Advertising	Analysing / Giving Opinions
15	Fact File – The Olympic Games	Information – Fact File	Supplying Questions for Answers
16	Election Time	Exposition – Brochure	Completing Profiles / Answering 'Who' Questions
17	The Big Bad Breath	Poetic – Poem	Cloze Activity / Providing Rhyming Words

Week	Title	Text Type	Comprehension Focus
18	Robot Attack	Exposition – Review	Completing a Table of Information / Multiple Choice
19	The Operation – A One-act Play	Narrative – Play	Ordering Sequence of Events / Providing Illustrations
20	What Is Colour?	Information – Scientific Facts	Recalling Detail / Sentence Matching
21	Camp Diary	Recount – Diary	Providing Information / Completing an Itinerary
22	A Roo Called Fred	Narrative Excerpt	True or False / Game
23	Headhunt	Information / Procedural – Game	Literal and Inferential Questioning
24	In an Emergency	Procedural – Instructions	Literal Questioning
25	Spaceport Passport	Information – Passport	Literal Questioning
26	The Giant Turnip	Narrative – Traditional Tale	Retelling a Story in Own Words
27	No Graffiti Here!	Exposition – Graffiti	Inferential Questioning
28	Cattle Dogs of Australia	Information – Factual Description	Recalling Detail / Identifying Parts of Speech
29	Madame Guessalot's Starscope	Exposition – Horoscopes	Answering 'Which' Questions
30	A Letter from the Goldfields	Recount – Letter	Literal and Inferential Questioning
31	Keeping an Eye on Things	Information – Report	Supplying Questions for Answers
32	A Bright Spark	Procedural – Experiment / Instructions	Literal Questioning
33	Rhyming Time	Poetic – Rhyming Slang	Matching Definitions / Inferential
34	Is He a Champion?	Recount – Newspaper Report	Literal and Inferential Questioning
35	Spidery Facts: Did You Know …?	Information – Factual Description	Literal Questioning / Labelling a Diagram

Now for the Bad News

Text Type: Narrative – Comic Strip

Answer these questions about the comic strip.

1. Who is the conversation between? ______
2. Where does the conversation take place? ______
3. What time of day is it? ______
4. Why is Mr Jones seeing the doctor? ______
5. What is the good news? ______
6. What is the bad news? ______
7. When did the doctor get the test results back? ______
8. What was the patient's reaction to the good news? ______
9. How many days does Mr Jones have to live? ______
10. Panel five of the comic strip has been written below in sentence form. Rewrite the sentences with the correct punctuation. The words in the balloons need to be enclosed in quotation marks.
    yes i m sorry consoled the doctor one day left it that s the good news what s the bad news asked the patient
    ______
    ______
    ______
11. Make up a different title for the comic strip.
    ______
12. Write a different ending for the comic strip.

Moving on

This is a 'Good News, Bad News' joke retold in comic-strip form. Write a joke you know in comic-strip form – if possible a 'Good News, Bad News' joke.

A Fable

A fable is a story that has a rule of behaviour that we should or should not follow.

This rule is called the moral of the story.

The Milkmaid and Her Pail

Every day a farmer's daughter had the chore of milking the cows. One day when the pail was full, she balanced the pail on her head as usual and set off for the dairy. As she strode along she began to daydream about the future.

"The milk in this pail will provide me with enough cream, which I will churn into butter. This butter I will sell at the market and with the money I will get, I will buy lots of eggs. When these eggs are hatched I will have my own chickens, and quite soon I will manage my own poultry farm. Then with the profits that I get when I sell the eggs and some of the fowls, I will buy myself a beautiful new outfit, which I shall wear to the country fair. At the fair all the young men will admire me and ask me on dates. But I shall have nothing to do with them. I shall toss my head ..." And she did.

Absorbed in her fantasies she forgot all about the pail on her head. The pail slipped off her head and all the milk was spilt. All her dreams vanished in an instant and the farmer's daughter was back exactly where she had started ... except, of course, there was no milk in the pail.

Text Type: Narrative – Fable

Answer these questions about the fable *The Milkmaid and Her Pail.*

1. What was the milkmaid's task?

2. How did she carry the milk pail to the dairy?

3. What did she plan to do after she sold the butter?

4. Why did the pail fall off the milkmaid's head?

5. What is the lesson to be learnt in the fable? Tick the correct alternative.
   - [ ] Don't put all your eggs in one basket.
   - [ ] Don't count your chickens before they hatch.
   - [ ] It's no use crying over spilt milk.

6. One version of this fable concludes with "… and all her fine castles in the air vanished in a moment". Which word in the last paragraph of the fable refers to "castles in the air"?

7. Find the word in the fable that means:

a task	______	**b** disappeared	______
c idolise	______	**d** hens	______
e gains	______	**f** engrossed	______
g purchase	______	**h** precisely	______

Moving on

Make up some excuses written by the milkmaid as to why she dropped the pail of milk. Try to make these humorous.

Famous Headlines

These headlines might have appeared in the newspapers, even if newspapers had not been invented when these things happened.

Titanic **Sinks in Atlantic: Iceberg Claims Many Victims**

QUEEN CLEOPATRA SUICIDES BY SNAKE BITE AFTER ROMAN ARMY DEFEATS EGYPTIAN FORCES

New Rock 'N' Roll Craze Sweeps Across Country

Kingsford-Smith and Ulm Cross Pacific in 83 Hours: Brisbane Crowd Goes Wild State Government Gives 5000 Pounds Reward

Strange Paintings Found in Cave by Three Boys: Paintings Thought to be 17 000 Years Old

Captain Cook Killed in Sandwich Islands. World Mourns Loss of Great Pacific Ocean Explorer

Engine-driven Kite Flies for First Time: Wright Brothers Craft in Air for 59 Seconds at 852 Feet

Sydney Town Low on Food: Colony May Fail

BREAKTHROUGH! NUCLEAR SUB *NAUTILUS* SURFACES AT NORTH POLE

Write the headlines that would have appeared above these stories.

1 ______________________________

Brisbane, Saturday. Huge crowds greeted the arrival of Captain Charles Kingsford-Smith and Charles Ulm after their record-breaking flight across the Pacific.

2 ______________________________

Sydney, Friday. Governor Phillip has warned the colony that it will need to ration food carefully if it is to survive the recent crop failure.

3 ______________________________

Los Angeles, Monday. Police are worried about the latest dance craze, which is resulting in teenagers dancing wildly in the streets.

4 ______________________________

Lascaux, France, Tuesday. A stray dog, which found its way into an opening in the ground, has led three boys to a dazzling gallery of cave paintings that have been held secret under the earth for the past 17 000 years.

5 ______________________________

London, Monday. The Cunard Line has released the shocking news that the mighty liner *Titanic* has sunk with great loss of life after striking an iceberg and sinking in the mid-Atlantic.

How much do the headlines tell us?

6 What was new about the Wright Brothers' kite? ______________________________

7 Why do you think Cleopatra took her own life? ______________________________

8 What would *Nautilus* have broken through to get to the North Pole? ______________________________

9 Where did Kingsford-Smith and Ulm first land their plane on Australian soil? ______________________________

10 Why was Captain Cook in Hawaii? ______________________________

Moving on

Make up your own headlines for a famous event from the past. How would you headline stories about:

1 Robin Hood's escape from the clutches of the Sheriff of Nottingham?
2 the first crossing of Australia by Burke and Wills?
3 Margaret Court becoming the first Australian woman to win at Wimbledon?

Ham and Pineapple Pizza

Ingredients

2 cups of self-raising flour
2 cups of grated cheese
1 cup of milk
1 cup of pineapple pieces
¾ cup of tomato paste
30 g of butter (chopped)
1 cup of ham (finely chopped)
¼ teaspoon of salt
1 sliced tomato
1 tablespoon of vegetable oil

Method

Step 1 Pre-heat oven to 220°C (425°F).

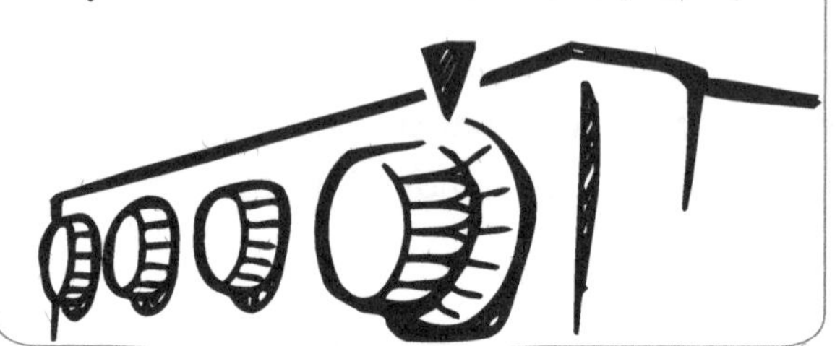

Step 2 Sift flour and salt into a mixing bowl. Rub butter into flour with tips of fingers.

Step 3 Add milk and mix. Knead into a soft dough. Add more milk if required.

Step 4 Roll dough onto a large pizza tray.

Step 5 Brush the oil onto the dough. Spread the tomato paste over the dough.

Step 6 Sprinkle the cheese over the paste. Place tomato slices on top.

Step 7 Top with ham and pineapple.

Step 8 Bake in oven for 20–25 minutes. Serve hot.

Note: Other toppings can be used; for example: mushrooms, bacon, green peppers, onions. Use your imagination.

WARNING: THIS ACTIVITY SHOULD ONLY BE DONE UNDER ADULT SUPERVISION.

Text Type: Procedural – Recipe

How well could you make a ham and pineapple pizza?

1. What type of flour is used?

2. How much tomato paste is used to make the pizza?

3. Which ingredients are dairy foods?

4. Why is the flour sifted?

5. With which ingredient is the flour sifted?

6. How is the butter added to the flour?

7. If the dough is difficult to knead, what should you do?

8. What would you use to roll out the dough?

9. What is the pizza cooked on?

10. What are the last two ingredients to be added?

11. In which step are the tomato slices added?

12. Why do you think the oven is pre-heated?

13. What do °C and °F mean?

14. What other toppings would you have on your pizza?

What was that word?

15. Find words in the recipe that mean:

a squeeze ______ **b** hacked ______ **c** needed ______

d sweep ______ **e** shredded ______ **f** cook ______

Moving on

1 Write out the recipe for one of your favourite foods. Combine your grade recipes into a Grade Recipe Book.

2 Try making the pizza in the recipe.

Weird and Wonderful

There are only three species of monotremes in the world – the long-beaked echidna and its cousin, the short-beaked echidna, and the platypus. Two of these are native to Australia and the other, the long-beaked echidna, is a resident of Papua New Guinea. These weird but wonderful creatures have the same characteristics as mammals in that they are warm-blooded, have a hair covering and suckle their young on milk. Because they lay eggs, they are classified differently from other mammals.

An extraordinary animal is the platypus, which features on our 20-cent coin. This duck-billed creature had scientists baffled when it was first discovered in 1797. It suckles its young as mammals do, lays eggs like a bird, has a head like a duck, a fur coat, sharp-clawed webbed feet and a flat tail like a beaver. The male platypus also has spurs on its hind legs that contain venom. Its webbed feet help make it a very good swimmer, as well as being very useful when digging in the banks of rivers and lakes. This timid creature builds its nest in a very intricate burrow system in the banks of the rivers and lakes it frequents. It is in this burrow that the two eggs are laid that are incubated by the female. Being amphibian, it is able to live on the land as well as in the water. While swimming, a flap of skin closes over its eyes and ears. The platypus uses its sensitive bill to seek out the worms, shrimps, snails and water insects it lives on.

The reverse side of our five-cent coin shows an echidna curled up into a ball. The echidna does this when it is threatened, and its spiny coat acts as its protection when it burrows down out of reach. Referred to as the 'Spiny Anteater', the echidna, which is toothless, uses its long, sticky tongue to penetrate ant and termite nests, which it breaks open with its strong claws. Growing to about the same length as the platypus, 60 to 70 centimetres, it can weigh up to seven kilograms. Like the platypus, the echidna has a spur on each of its ankles, but these are non-venomous. The echidna doesn't have a fixed abode but rather shelters wherever it can find a place – under bushes, in hollow logs and in caves. Only one soft-shelled egg is laid and the young is suckled inside the mother's pouch. When born, it does not have spines and is carried in the pouch until the growing quills become too uncomfortable for the mother. This occurs at about three months of age.

Text Type: Information – Factual Description

The answers to the crossword are all in the extract 'Weird and Wonderful'.

ACROSS

3 The platypus lays its eggs in a ______.

4 Nourishment for the young of the platypus and echidna.

8 The echidna and platypus are native to this country.

10 Term given to an animal that is warm-blooded, has hair and produces milk.

11 This monotreme has no regular home.

12 Baby echidnas are carried in this.

14 An egg-laying mammal.

DOWN

1 A synonym for 'spines'.

2 Which type of beaked echidna can be found in Papua New Guinea?

5 The echidna is sometimes called this.

6 Had early scientists confused.

7 Mammals are ______ blooded.

8 Able to live on land and in water.

9 A poisonous secretion.

13 Contains venom on a male platypus.

Using plasticine, playdough or clay, make a model of either the platypus or the echidna. Make an information card to go with it.

Up, Up and Away

"Man has always dreamed of being able to fly."

This timeline shows some of the advancements made in flight from 1783 to 1969.

1783 French brothers Joseph and Jacques Montgolfier flew a hot-air balloon over a distance of 8 kilometres for 25 minutes. The balloon was made of paper! The basket carried a duck, a rooster and a sheep.

1849 Sir George Cayley, a British aeronautical engineer, designed and built a glider that flew a man across a Yorkshire valley.

1852 French engineer and inventor Henri Giffard flew 29 kilometres at a speed of about 10 kilometres per hour in a cigar-shaped airship powered by a steam engine. The airship could only be steered in calm conditions.

1903 On 17 December the Wright brothers – Orville and Wilbur – made the world's first successful flight in a heavier-than-air-craft. Each brother made two flights that day, the longest by Wilbur, who covered a distance of 260 metres in 59 seconds.

1907 A rotating wing aircraft – one of the first helicopters, designed by Frenchman Paul Cornu – rose 60 metres above the ground.

1919 British aviators John Alcock and Arthur Brown collected a prize of $50 000 when they made the first non-stop flight across the Atlantic.

1947 Released from the belly of a bomber, the ***Bell X1***, piloted by Captain Charles Yeager, broke the sound barrier (approximately 1223 kilometres per hour), which is referred to scientifically as 'Mach 1'.

1961 Soviet cosmonaut Yuri Gagarin became the first man in space when his spacecraft ***Vostok 1*** orbited Earth on 12 April. The flight lasted one hour and 48 minutes.

1963 In June, Valentina Tereshkova, who was a textile worker before becoming a Soviet cosmonaut, became the first woman in space when she orbited Earth 48 times in her ***Vostok 6*** fight.

1969 "That's one small step for man, one giant leap for mankind." These words were spoken on 20 July by American astronaut Neil Armstrong as he set foot on the moon's surface – the first person to do so. His fellow astronauts on the ***Apollo 11*** mission were Edwin Aldrin and Michael Collins.

Text Type: Information – Timeline

Read each statement and tick whether it is true or false.

	True	False
1 There was a time span of eight years from when man first flew into space until man first stepped on the moon.	☐	☐
2 One of the first helicopters was designed by Frenchman Paul Cornu.	☐	☐
3 American astronaut Valentina Tereshkova was the first woman in space.	☐	☐
4 The Montgolfier brothers were pioneers in the development of hot-air balloons.	☐	☐
5 In 1849, Britisher Sir George Cayley tested a glider across the Simpson Desert in Australia.	☐	☐
6 In 1783, a balloon flight successfully carried a duck, a rooster and a donkey.	☐	☐
7 Neil Armstrong, Edwin Aldrin and Michael Collins were members of the *Apollo 11* mission to the moon.	☐	☐
8 In 1919, Britisher John Alcock made a solo flight across the Atlantic.	☐	☐

9 Write your own 'True or False' statement from the information on the previous page. Tick whether it is true or false.

______________________________________ ☐ ☐

____

10 What do you think Neil Armstrong meant when he said, "That's one small step for man, one giant leap for mankind"?

____

____

____

Moving on

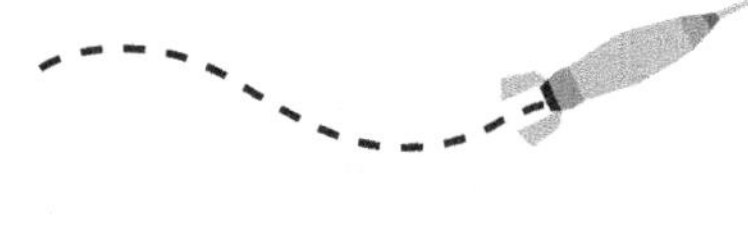

Design a paper plane. See who can fly their plane the furthest.

Top 20

This Week	Last Week	Song	Artist/s	No. Weeks in
1	1	'How Much is that Dingo in the Window?'	Uluru Band	6
2	5	'Bridge over Sydney Harbour'	The Coathangers	5
3	3	'Leave Your Akubra on'	Greg Norman and the Sharks	8
4	9	'Give Me a Home on the Gold Coast'	Holden Drivers	4
5	*	'Koala's in the Cradle'	The Kelly Gang	1
6	8	'Crocodile Dundee Rock'	Paul and Linda Hogan	11
7	2	'A Touch of Surfers Paradise'	The Rockaroos	13
8	29	'Jumpin' Jack Kangaroo'	Jacko and the Energisers	3
9	14	'Blue Suede Thongs'	Uluru Band	5
10	23	'Click Go the Bails'	Ricky Ponting and the Cricketers	3
11	38	'Rock Around Uluru'	Uluru Band	2
12	25	'Walk like an Emu'	MCG & the Whackers	4
13	13	'Australian Pie'	The Downunders	10
14	4	'Gumbush'	The Kelly Gang	12
15	7	'Let Me Be your Koala Bear'	The Rockaroos	9
16	11	'Surfin' in the Bells Beach Classic'	Great Australian Bight	9
17	*	'Twinkle Twinkle Southern Cross'	Eureka Stockade	1
18	12	'Puff the Magic Possum'	The BBQ Boys	8
19	15	'Roll over Grant Hackett'	The Waltzing Matildas	7
20	6	'She'll Be Comin' Round the Snowy Mountains'	Bill Kosciusko and the Peaks	12

*** FIRST WEEK IN THE CHARTS**

Text Type: Information – Lists

Answer these questions about the music chart.

1. How many songs are in the same position this week as last week? ____________
2. Which songs are the latest to be released?

   ____________ ____________

3. Which artists have more than one hit on the chart?

   ____________ ____________ ____________

4. How many songs on the chart were not in the Top 20 last week? ____________
5. Which song has been in the charts for the longest time?

   ____

6. Name one song that has decreased in popularity since last week and one song that has increased in popularity.

   ____

7. What do all the songs have in common?

   ____

8. Name two songs that refer to locations in Australia.

   ____

   ____

9. Why is it appropriate that the group The Coathangers sings the song 'Bridge over Sydney Harbour'? ____________
10. All the songs on this chart are well-known songs that have been changed to give them an Australian flavour, for example: 'Blue Suede Shoes' has been changed to 'Blue Suede Thongs'. List three other original song titles.

    ____

    ____

    ____

Moving on

Create your own 'Aussie' song title and artist or group. Design a cover for the CD.

Happy Harry's Hamburger Heaven

The Harryburger

A BIG 250-gram better-beef patty topped with lettuce, onion, garlic, chilli, tomato and Harry's special surprise sauce between a scrumptious lightly-burnt bun. One bite from the Harryburger and your friends will be so jealous they will not want to talk to you for 24 hours. $4.95

The Jumboburger

For the really big eater a huge two-kilogram fatty beef patty topped with a chicken fillet and peanut butter, stuck inside a loaf of bread. Get your teeth into this one, if you can get your mouth around it! $9.95

Harry's Dietburger

For the diet-conscious eater a one-millimetre thin, really thin, slice of beef with a limp cabbage leaf, sultanas, fruit salad topped with fresh (well, almost) yoghurt. Energy and healthy living all in a low-joule crispy wafer. Be the thinnest on your block with the thinnest hamburger in the world. Valued at $3.95, but for you a special at $2.00.

The Fryburger

No fuss! No frills! Just a handful of crisp fries (the cooks have been asked to wash their hands, so no worries there) swamped in lashings of tomato sauce and 10 grams of salt, all in a crispy bun. Enjoy with a FREE litre of Harry's delicious ice-cold water. All this for a cheap $2.80.

The Oceanburger

Filled with fresh fish from the mouth of the Grunge River topped with slices of sea snail, raw seaweed and our special tangy frog's liver sauce, enclosed in a chewy bun sprinkled with stale sesame seeds. With bones just $4.25. Without bones $12.95.

The Kiddieburger

For the tiny tots. A 50-gram patty of freshly ground beef topped with raspberry jam and hundreds and thousands between two slices of fairy cake. Watch the littlies gulp this one down and come back for more. $3.95

Special Family Pack

Be the only one on your block to order a Jumboburger, Harry's 'Fried to a Crisp' fries, and a big 500 millilitres of mouthwash for just $10.95.

Harry's is at one convenient location: 184 Hartwell Highway, Brentwood

Restaurant review

Our reviewer, Carly Carnivore, has written the following report on Harry's Hamburger Heaven. Some of the words have been left out of the report.
Fill them in.

I visited the new hamburger restaurant in (1)________________. Harry's Hamburger Heaven has all the (2)________________ you can think of; some for the healthy and some for the (3)________________. He even has a Dietburger for those who would like to get (4)________________ but be careful of the (5)________________, which is not very fresh.

The most expensive hamburger is the (6)________________, which contains plenty of (7)________________ but there are no (8)________________ to catch in your throat. Just a little less expensive is the (9)________________, which is made for the (10)________________ eaters. You have to have a big (11)________________ just to get your teeth into it.

For the children there is the (12)________________, which is unusual because spread on top is (13)________________ jam and (14)________________ and thousands. Perhaps this is just (15)________________ for the kiddies because I don't think (16)________________ would like this one. To go with all of Harry's hamburgers are the 'Fried to a Crisp' (17)________________, which are OK if you like badly (18)________________ chips. Harry's could be just the place to (19)________________ the family if you want to put them off hamburgers for the rest of their (20)________________.

Moving on

Make up a list of the food items from Harry's that you would like to buy for your worst enemy. Work out how much they would cost, then make sure you find a way to make the other person pay.

How to Eat a Meat Pie

You have to be an expert to eat a meat pie properly. Wash your hands before you start. Remove the pie from its bag, taking care because it could burn your fingers. Place the pie on top of the bag and hold it from below to protect your hand.

Make sure that you put plenty of tomato sauce on your pie. This makes your pie a much nicer colour and it helps to make it taste better too. Lean forward. This is important because you do not want to get pie or sauce on your clothes. Stand with your legs apart so that no drips can get on your shoes. If you are sitting, make sure that your knees are well apart. You do not want to spoil things when you are watching a sports event.

Now comes the eating part. Nibble the pastry around the front edge of the pie until you can see the meat inside. You might have to keep blowing on the pie to make sure it is not hot enough to burn your mouth or tongue. Keep your eye on the sauce to make sure that it is not moving around too much on the top of the pie and dripping down the sides.

When the front of the pie has been eaten away, you can look inside to see if the filling is firm or runny. If it is runny you must make sure that you hold the pie at an angle so that the meat cannot run out. You might have to lick away some of the sauce if it looks like it will run over the back edge and onto your fingers. Runny meat can be sucked out if that is what you like to do. This means that you will have to eat the pie crust at the same time as you are sucking out the meat.

As you are eating, work your way down and across the pie just as if you were working your way down a page in a book. Don't forget to keep licking any sauce that might slide off the back or sides of the pie.

When you reach the last mouthful, you can hold your head back, open your mouth wide and drop the last of the pie in. Lick your fingers to make sure you get the rest of the crumbs and any bits of sauce that might be there.

Text Type: Procedural – Instructions

In step ...

The following steps for eating a meat pie are out of order. Use the numbers 1 to 10 to show which order you think is correct. If you are working with a partner, work out a strategy between you for completing this exercise.

_____ Lean forward.

_____ Look inside the pie.

_____ Lick off the sauce that runs towards the back edge.

_____ Remove the pie from its bag.

_____ Work your way backwards and forwards across the pie.

_____ Drop the last of the pie into your mouth.

_____ Nibble the pastry at the front.

_____ Stand with your legs apart or sit with your knees apart.

_____ Put the pie on top of the bag.

_____ Blow on the pie.

Why should you ...

1. ... keep your legs or knees apart?

____

2. ... look inside the pie?

____

3. ... blow on the pie?

____

4. ... put plenty of sauce on your pie?

____

5. ... lick your fingers?

____

Moving on

Describe your method for eating some other food. Perhaps it could be a Vegemite sandwich, a bowl of ice-cream or a coffee scroll.

The Wild Colonial Boy

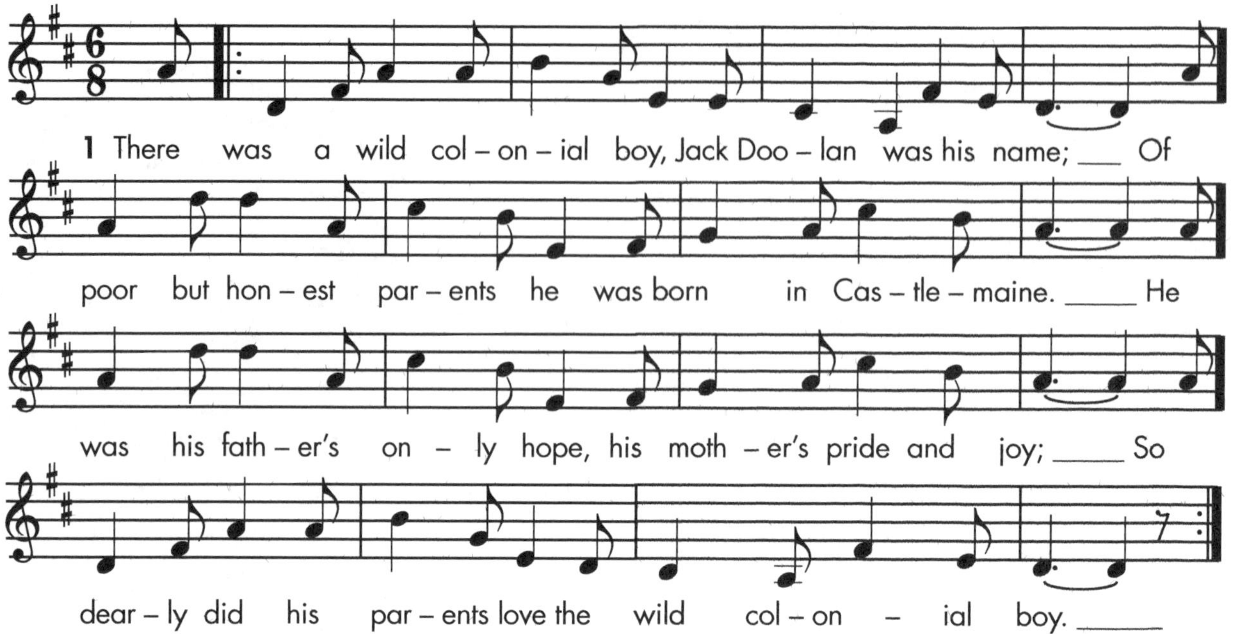

2 He was scarcely sixteen years of age when he left his father's home,
And through Australia's sunny clime a bushranger did roam.
He robbed those wealthy squatters, and their stock he did destroy,
A terror to the rich man was the wild colonial boy.

3 In sixty one this daring youth commenced his wild career;
With a heart that knew no danger, no foe man did he fear.
He held the Beechworth mail coach up and robbed Judge Macoboy,
Who trembling cold gave up his gold to the wild colonial boy.

4 One day as he was riding the mountain side along,
A-list'ning to that kookaburra's happy laughing song,
He spied three mounted troopers, Kelly, Davis and Fitzroy,
A-riding up to capture him, the wild colonial boy.

5 "Surrender now, Jack Doolan, for y'see there's three to one.
Surrender in the Queen's high name, you daring highway man!"
But he drew a pistol from his belt and spun it like a toy:
"I'll fight but never surrender," cried the wild colonial boy.

6 He fired at Trooper Kelly and brought him to the ground,
And in return from Davis received a mortal wound;
All shattered through the jaws he lay still firing at Fitzroy,
And that's the way they captured him, the wild colonial boy.

Text Type: Narrative – Song

Find the answers to the questions in the wordsearch below.
Colour the squares containing the answer as indicated in brackets.

What was the given name of the wild colonial boy? (red)

Where was the wild colonial boy born? (green)

What would the wild colonial boy never do? (orange)

What was the name of the judge he robbed? (dark blue)

How old was Jack Doolan when he left home? (pink)

What were Kelly, Davis and Fitzroy? (yellow)

Which mail coach did Jack hold up? (light blue)

Who shot the wild colonial boy? (purple)

Which word in the song is a synonym for 'highway man'? (brown)

Which trooper did the wild colonial boy shoot? (black)

THE WORDS CAN GO ACROSS, BACKWARDS, UP OR DOWN AND DIAGONALLY.

E	A	C	S	R	E	P	O	O	R	T	B	F	M
N	S	B	E	E	C	H	W	O	R	T	H	A	E
I	S	I	Q	A	D	R	D	Q	P	N	C	E	S
A	U	J	X	N	V	K	Q	X	L	O	Z	I	O
M	R	A	L	T	G	Y	G	R	B	U	V	E	K
E	R	K	T	I	E	T	F	O	L	A	O	J	I
L	E	X	C	T	G	E	Y	P	D	O	G	R	S
T	N	H	S	A	D	X	N	W	K	E	L	L	Y
S	D	Z	M	H	J	F	Z	W	L	P	V	N	L
A	E	T	R	E	G	N	A	R	H	S	U	B	B
C	R	Y	M	U	M	O	N	S	C	T	U	B	R

Make up a wordsearch on a theme of your choice.

Comprehension Focus: Finding Answers in a Wordsearch / Recalling Detail

Week 11

Big

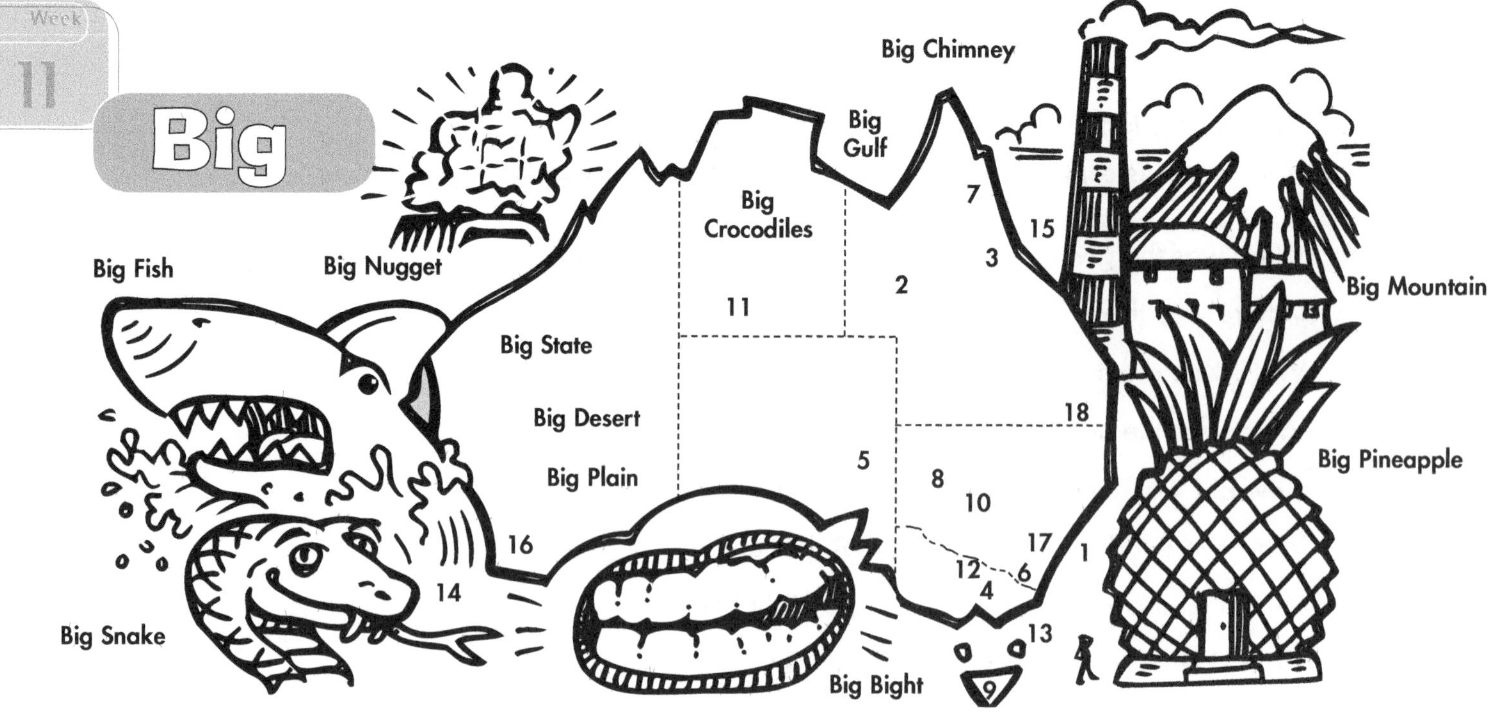

1 **Big Coathanger** Sydney Harbour Bridge. Taking nine years to build, it opened in 1932. Weighing 52 732 tonnes, it is 509 metres long.

2 **Big Chimney** The MIM chimney, Mt Isa, Queensland, is 270 metres high.

3 **Big Road** National Highway (No. 1), clockwise from the north of Cairns to Darwin, is 12 390 kilometres long.

4 **Big Building** The Eureka Tower in Melbourne is 300 metres tall and has 88 storeys.

5 **Big Lake** Lake Eyre, SA. This salt lake covers an area of 9300 square kilometres.

6 **Big Mountain** Mt Kosciuszko, NSW. Part of the Snowy Mountains Range, it is 2228 metres high.

7 **Big Snake** An Amethystine Python shot near Cairns in 1948 was 7.6 metres long.

8 **Big River** The Darling River, NSW, runs a course of 2739 kilometres.

9 **Big Island** Tasmania is the 24th largest island in the world and covers an area of 67 896 square kilometres.

10 **Big Dish** Parkes CSIRO Radio Telescope. The dish is 64 metres in diameter.

11 **Big Rock** Uluru is the biggest monolith (single rock) in the world and is 335 metres high and 9 kilometres around the base.

12 **Big Nugget** 'The Welcome Stranger', found at Moliagul, Victoria, in 1869, yielded 69.9 kilograms of pure gold.

13 **Big Beach** The Ninety-Mile Beach extends from Port Albert to Lakes Entrance on the eastern coast of Victoria.

14 **Big Fish** A white pointer shark caught off Ledge Point, WA, in 1984 was 5.9 metres long.

15 **Big Reef** The Great Barrier Reef is the greatest coral structure in the world and covers a distance of about 2000 kilometres.

16 **Big Belt** The conveyor belt between Mt Saddleback Mine and the Worsley Refinery near Collie, WA, is in two flights – one 31 kilometres long; the other 20 kilometres long.

17 **Big House** Parliament House – situated on Capital Hill, Canberra's new Parliament House was opened by the Queen in May 1988.

18 **Big Pineapple** This popular tourist attraction is near Nambour in Queensland.

Text Type: Information – Factual Description

See if you can write some BIG answers.

1. How many states and territories does the National Highway travel through? ____________

2. **Match 'em up.**

   All the numbers below are lengths in metres. Match each number with a feature by ruling lines.

2 739 000 •	• Eureka Tower
64 •	• MIM Chimney
2228 •	• White pointer shark
300 •	• CSIRO Radio Telescope
270 •	• Darling River
5.9 •	• Mt Kosciuszko
335 •	• National Highway
12 390 000 •	• Uluru

3. In which state or territory would you find these towns or cities?

   a Port Albert ____________ **b** Cairns ____________

   c Parkes ____________ **d** Mt Isa ____________

4. In which state would you find these features?

a  ____________ **b**  ____________

c 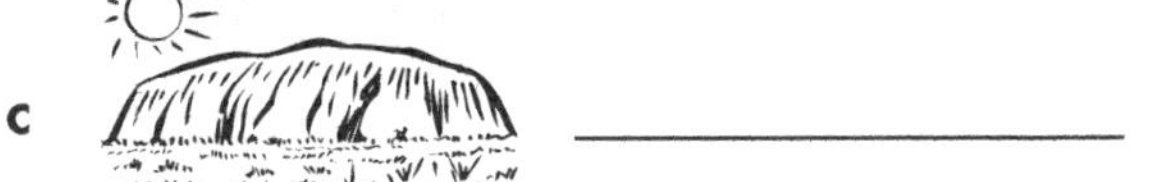 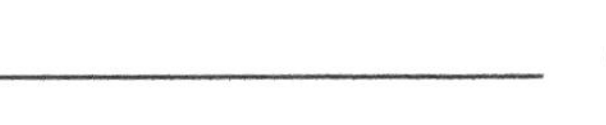 ____________ **d**  ____________

e   ____________ **f**  ____________

g  ____________ **h**  ____________

Moving on

Make a list of other BIG things in Australia.

or

Make a list of words that mean BIG.

The Magic Jar

One day while digging in the backyard, a poor man came upon an enormous earthenware jar. He dug around the jar so that he could remove it from the __(1)__ and took it inside for his wife to clean. She scrubbed the outside of the jar, but when she began to scrub inside with a brush, the jar filled with brushes. No matter how many she took out, others kept taking their place. The man and his __(2)__ decided to sell the brushes, and as they had an inexhaustible supply of __(3)__, it was not long before they became quite wealthy.

One day the man accidentally dropped a coin, which fell into the jar. Straight away the brushes disappeared and their place was taken by coins. No matter how many __(4)__ were removed from the jar, they were always replaced by more coins. The man and his wife were now very __(5)__ indeed.

Living with the man and his wife was his grandfather. He was very __(6)__ and feeble and as there was very little that he could do, he was instructed to shovel the money from the __(7)__. He did this every day, but when he grew tired, he would stop __(8)__. The man was annoyed at this as he wanted as much money as he could lay his hands on. He would shout at the old grandfather and call him a "lazy good-for-nothing".

Finally, one day, the old grandfather's strength gave out. He collapsed and died. As he collapsed he fell into the jar. Immediately, the coins disappeared and the jar was full of __(9)__ grandfathers. The man had to pull them out. Each time he pulled out a dead grandfather, it was replaced by another. The man also needed to have all the grandfathers buried, and it was not very long before all the money from the jar was used up on coffins and funerals. No money, but a jar full of dead grandfathers! In his frustration, the man kicked the jar and it broke into __(10)__. All the dead grandfathers disappeared. No more dead grandfathers but the man was as poor as he'd been before he __(11)__ the jar.

Traditional Chinese Folk Tale

Text Type: Narrative – Traditional Tale

In this cloze activity, choose the best word from each box to match the numbered spaces in the story. Write the word on the line next to the box.

1. jar ground shelf tree ______
2. dog brushes jar wife ______
3. brushes jars wives coins ______
4. jars grandfathers coins brushes ______
5. unhappy clean poor wealthy ______
6. young fast old strong ______
7. floor ground jar bank ______
8. working dancing eating sleeping ______
9. lazy feeble old dead ______
10. grandfathers jars pieces tears ______
11. Write three different words that could be used to complete space (11).

    ______

12. How would you have solved the problem of the dead grandfathers without breaking the jar?

    ______

Moving on

Write a new ending for the story *The Magic Jar*.

Children's Week

The children at Montross Primary School celebrate Children's Week with a week of special activities. Here is the timetabled program for one of the Grade 6 days.

Letter Day – 'G' Day

Monday, 26 October

Remember: Our grade's letter is 'G'. Come dressed as something beginning with the letter G.

9:00 a.m.	**Introduction to Children's Week.**
9:05 a.m.	**Judging and Presentation of Awards for Letter Day:** A certificate and 50 house points to the best-dressed girl and boy.
9:15 a.m.	**International News:** Bring news items and cuttings from around the world and present them to the grade. These will be placed on the World News Board. This will be held daily for the week.
9:30 a.m.	**'Clothes Maketh the Man':** A cooperative talk session. What do you think of this well-known saying? Be prepared to report back to your grade. (Groups of 3–5.)
9:50 a.m.	**Maths (your favourite):** Skeleton letters and word equations
10:15 a.m.	**Make a Passport:** For next week's 'Trip around the World'. You'll also be receiving your injections. (Just joking!)
10:30 a.m.	**Morning Recess**
10:45 a.m.	**Baby Photo Competition:** Fifty house points to the person who identifies the most babies. Give your photo to Mr Brown prior to Children's Week. Don't show your photo to anyone.
11:15 a.m.	**Snail Races:** Start training your snails now so that they will be in peak fitness. Fifty house points and a certificate to the winning owner. See if your snail can beat last year's record of 12 minutes and 15 seconds set by 'The Terminator'.
11:45 a.m.	**Super Spectacular Sandwich Competition:** Make before school. To win the prize you must eat your sandwich. Fifty house points and a certificate to the winner.
12:00	**Continue eating your sandwich … if you can!**
12:15 p.m.	**Lunch Recess**
1:15 p.m.	**BMX Rally:** Make sure your bikes are in good mechanical order. Fifty house points and a certificate to the winning boy and girl.
2:15 p.m.	**Afternoon Recess**
2:30 p.m.	**Trivia Afternoon** Five teams of six students. Who will be the winning team? Will it be 'The Brainy Bunch' or 'The Quizoids'? Or will it be 'The Smarties' or 'Four Men and a Baby'? Or will it be 'The Braindeads'? Fifty house points and a certificate to each winning member.
3:25 p.m.	**Tidy up and discuss tomorrow's activities.**
3:30 p.m.	**Dismissal**

Have a great day!

Text Type: Exposition – Program

Look at the program for Letter Day and answer these questions.

1. Which activities are on at the following times?

   a 1:30 p.m. ______________ **b** 10:05 a.m. ______________

   c 3:15 p.m. ______________ **d** 11:20 a.m. ______________

   e 9:20 a.m. ______________ **f** 10:55 a.m. ______________

2. What is the teacher's name? ______________

3. What kinds of newspaper cuttings should the children collect?

   ____

4. How many certificates will be given out on Letter Day? ______________

5. Who won last year's Snail Race? ______________

6. What is the award for winning the BMX Rally?

   ____

7. What do the children have to do to win the Baby Photo Competition?

   ____

8. How many children are in the grade? ______________

9. Name three things the children could dress up as.

   ______________ ______________ ______________

10. Place the numbers 1 to 6 in the boxes in the order the activities occurred during the day.

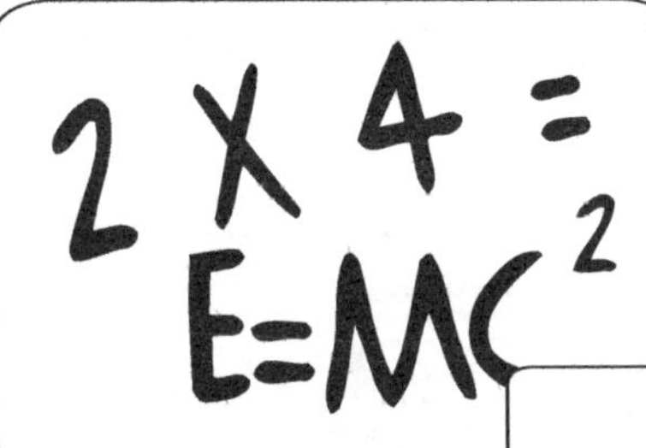

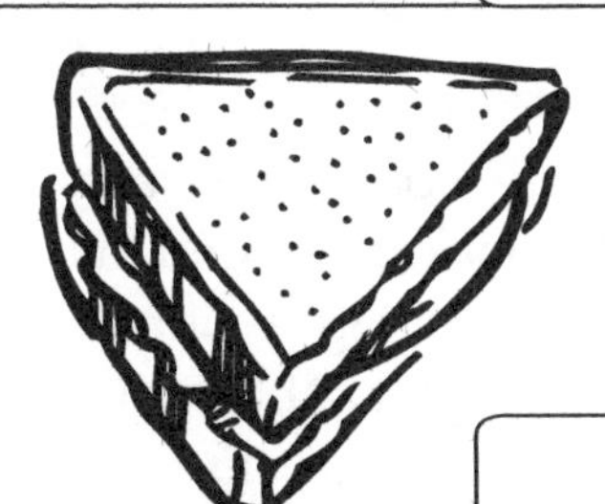

Moving on

Design a poster advertising Children's Week.

For Sale

Mansion for Sale

All you could wish for in a house. Only 500 years old. Eight bedrooms, four with BIR. Main bedroom complete with ensuite, toilet and shower. Three extra toilets complete with trapdoor for removing unwanted guests. Two bathrooms, one up, one down, with bath, washbasin and built-in bat perches. Room for more bats in the spacious attic. Dining room. Library with revolving bookshelves and EC. Fully furnished with dusty furniture and attractively draped with cobwebs. All windows fitted with locked shutters. Very attractive dungeon complete with comfortable silk-lined coffin. Kitchen with WO and HP, practically unused. Laboratory comes with fully fitted electricals. Only one previous owner – Dr Frankenstein. Attractively priced at $600 000.

Ship for Sale

Barque Endeavour. Slightly used. Originally a coal ship. Extensively renovated. Length 90 feet, beam 15 feet. Recently returned from round-theworld voyage. Masts of best Baltic timber. Sails in good condition; some patches. Eight cannons in good working order, one small pivoting cannon; good supply of cannonballs and grapeshot. Two longboats in very good condition equipped with eight oars each. Experienced crew; 28 ordinary sailors, bosun, cook and two cabin boys. Spacious between decks, modern galley with all pots, pans and cutlery, hammocks for all crew of best canvas in excellent condition. Captain's cabin (recently occupied by Mr J. Cook) has all modern conveniences including desk, solid wooden cabinets, toilet and brass candle holders. Buyers can also purchase navigation instruments: compass, sextant, callipers, etc; will separate. Asking price: 1250 pounds. Will accept cash or bank note. Apply Admiral Beattie, Liverpool Shipyards, any time during working hours.

Forest

Rainforest, 1200 hectares, some trees over 200 years old, heavy rainfall area, home to many kinds of birds and animals. Soil averages 10 cm deep, ideal for logging, housing or farmland. Council permit to clear and put on electricity and water. First to see will buy. Sell for $100 000. Terms 10% down and balance within 30 days. Contact owner, I. L. Sawyer on (09) 753 297 or Agents Choppit, Cuttit and Burnitt, 18 Reckitts Road, Roonation, Ph. (09) 753 361

Horse for Sale

Mountain pony, 12 hands high, only eight years old, brown with black mane and tail, used mainly for cattle mustering. Helped recapture the colt from Old Regret. Able to jump most obstacles, obedient and strong, one owner, bred from wild bush horses. Worth 1000 pounds to owner but will sell for 750 pounds. Owner must sell as going to Queensland with friend for mustering. Contact J. Reilly c/o Corryong Post Office or ask for the Man from Snowy River at Court House Hotel.

The following checklists were drawn up by people wanting to buy some of the things mentioned in the classified ads. Put a tick next to the items mentioned in the ads. Put a cross next to the items not mentioned in the ads.

House

At least four bedrooms
Bathroom
Two toilets
Two storeys
Old style
Games room
Clean
Cellar
Unfurnished
Swimming pool
Separate dining room
Modern kitchen
No more than half a million dollars

Ship

Proven over long voyages
Good masts
Good sails
Four longboats
No more than 25 crew
Well equipped captain's cabin
At least 100 feet long
Galley with crockery and cutlery
Navigation instruments included
Cabin boy
Price no more than 1500 pounds

Horse

Dark colour
Strong
Obedient
Male
Bush-horse bred
No more than 12 hands
No more than 6 years old
Good jumper
No more than 500 pounds

Land

At least 1500 hectares
No wildlife
Suitable for forest
Trees for timber
Deep soil
Council permit to cut trees
Good rainfall
Pay no more than $700 000

Moving on

1 Do you think the person wanting the ship bought the *Endeavour*?

2 Do you think the person wanting the house would think Dr Frankenstein's house was suitable?

3 Was the person who wanted to buy some forest land interested in conserving the wildlife?

4 Was the mountain pony suitable for the person wanting to buy a horse?

Fact File – The Olympic Games

Oldest competitor: Oscar Swahn of Sweden competed in the Antwerp Games (1920) at the age of 73 and won a sliver medal for shooting.

The first modern Olympics:

- 311 athletes from 13 countries
- Nine sports contested, consisting of 43 events
- **James Connolly** from the USA became the first Olympic Champion of the Modern Games, winning the long jump.
- Australian **Edwin Flack** won the 800 metres and the 1500 metres.

The torch relay was introduced at the Berlin Games in 1936. A total of 3000 runners carried the torch across Europe from Olympia (Greece) to Berlin.

The Olympic Flag was first raised at the 7th Olympics in Antwerp (Belgium) in 1920.

1896 Athens, Greece
1900 Paris, France
1904 St Louis, USA
1908 London, England
1912 Stockholm, Sweden
1920 Antwerp, Belgium

1924 Paris, France
1928 Amsterdam, Holland
1932 Los Angeles, USA
1936 Berlin, Germany
1948 London, England

1952 Helsinki, Finland
1956 Melbourne, Australia
1960 Rome, Italy
1964 Tokyo, Japan
1968 Mexico City, Mexico

1972 Munich, West Germany
1976 Montreal, Canada
1980 Moscow, USSR
1984 Los Angeles, USA
1988 Seoul, South Korea

1992 Barcelona, Spain
1996 Atlanta, USA
2000 Sydney, Australia
2004 Athens, Greece
2008 Beijing, China
2012 London, England

Most gold medals:

- US swimmer **Michael Phelps** won a total of 14 gold medals at the 2004 and 2008 Games.
- Finnish athlete **Paavo Nurmi**, Soviet gymnast **Larissa Latynina,** US athlete **Carl Lewis** and US swimmer **Mark Spitz** all won nine gold medals.

Most Olympics: Italian show jumper **Raimondo D'Inzeo** rode in eight Olympics from 1948 to 1976, winning six medals.

Most gold medals in the one event: Only two competitors have won the same event four times:

- **Al Oerter** (USA) won the discus throw from 1956 to 1968.
- **Carl Lewis** (USA) won the long jump from 1984 to 1996.

Most medals: Gymnast **Larissa Latynina** (USSR) won 18 Olympic medals – nine gold, five silver and four bronze.

Most gold medals at one Games: **Michael Phelps** (USA) won eight gold medals for swimming at Beijing in 2008.

For this exercise the answers are given. Your task is to provide questions to match from the information given in the Fact File.

Example: **Answer:** **Gymnastics.**
Question: **In which sport did Larissa Latynina win her 18 Olympic medals?**

1. Answer: Antwerp, Belgium

   Question: ______________________________

2. Answer: 1928

   Question: ______________________________

3. Answer: Michael Phelps

   Question: ______________________________

4. Answer: Athens

   Question: ______________________________

5. Answer: Nine

   Question: ______________________________

6. Answer: London, England

   Question: ______________________________

7. Answer: 28 years

   Question: ______________________________

8. Write your own answer from the Fact File. Then write a question to match.

   Answer: ______________________________

   Question: ______________________________

1. Draw an Olympic flag showing the correct colours.
2. Find out what the Olympic flag symbolises.

Election Time

The Grade 6 students at Montross Primary School were studying our political systems. A mock election was held between the two classes. Below is a profile sheet on the candidates as prepared by one of the classes.

Know Your Candidate

KELLY JARVIS
Leader of the AFP

Leading Australians into the future
VOTE 1 – AFP

A very talented lady in many areas is Kelly Jarvis, leader of the AFP and soon to be the first woman Prime Minister of Australia. After breezing through secondary school, she went on to graduate with honours in Law and Economics. She worked for several years as a company taxation consultant before moving into politics. Married with three children, she has always lived in Montross. Outside politics, she enjoys going to the theatre, playing sport and spending time with her family. Number one ticket-holder for the Collingwood Football Club, she attends matches whenever she gets the opportunity. A dynamic but fair person with outstanding leadership qualities. Has set a new trend with her polka-dot dresses. 41 years old.

ELISHA MURRAY
Your future Minister for the Environment

For a cleaner, safer environment
VOTE 1 – AFP

Elisha Murray has achieved a lot in her lifetime. After graduating with Honours in Arts and Social Studies, she worked in journalism before branching into politics. A member of the World Environment Committee, she is a tireless worker for this cause and says, "I am committed to devoting my life to help save our world." A sporting enthusiast (in her younger days she represented Victoria in basketball), she finds time to coach local junior teams and says she is "an avid Collingwood fan". Her husband is a noted sports commentator and they have two children – Wesley and Lucinda. 39 years old.

DEINIOL OWEN
Your future Minister for Education

Our future lies in Education – for the best education possible
VOTE 1 – AFP

Known as the "quiet achiever", Deiniol has built up an impressive record. A top student all the way through school, he graduated with a Masters Degree in Education. A brilliant teacher, he became the youngest principal ever when he took over Montross Primary School at the age of 25. Married with three children, he lives in Mount Dandenong and is a very active sportsperson, still playing football, tennis and golf. He played over 50 League games for Melbourne, which he supports. He knows education and is committed to improving the standards in our schools. 37 years old.

VOTE 1 – AFP **LEADING AUSTRALIANS INTO THE FUTURE**

Text Type: Exposition – Brochure

Complete a profile for each of the three candidates.

Surname ______	Surname ______	Surname ______
First name ______	First name ______	First name ______
Age ______	Age ______	Age ______
Marital status ______	Marital status ______	Marital status ______
Number of children______	Number of children______	Number of children______
First job______	First job______	First job______
Interests______	Interests______	Interests______

Write on the line the name of the candidate who ...

1. ... graduated in Law and Economics ______
2. ... is 39 years old ______
3. ... lives in Mount Dandenong ______
4. ... played basketball for Victoria ______
5. ... has two children ______
6. ... wears polka-dot dresses ______
7. ... is married to a sports commentator ______
8. ... would be a taxation expert ______
9. ... supports the Melbourne Football Club______
10. ... enjoys the theatre ______
11. ... was a school principal ______
12. ... is involved with environmental groups______

Moving on

Pretend that you (or a friend) are a candidate for a mock election and write a profile for yourself (or your friend) including all the relevant information.

Surname ______	Number of children ______
First name ______	First job ______
Age ______	Interests ______
Marital status ______	______

The Big Bad Breath

For all those folks who think they know
That wolves and pigs just do not know
How to get along together
At any time, in any weather,
Just listen to this tale of hope
Don't sit there like a sullen dope.
We know those pigs had had it rough,
From all that wolfish huff and puff,
But don't forget one pig was saved
Despite the fact that Wolfie raved.
The story that the great big snot
Ended in the piglet's pot
Was only just a vicious rumour
To give it all a touch of humour (!?).
What follows is how they made amends
And are now considered best of friends.

After Wolf had destroyed the digs
Belonging to the other pigs,
He huffed away at the house of brick
Until it made him fairly sick.
While through the keyhole the pig could spy
The efforts of this Wolfie guy.
But what really scared him half to death
Was the terrible smell of Wolfie's breath.
And when at last the wolf got weary,
The pig said, "Excuse me Wolfie, dearie,
Your breath smells absolutely rotten.
Tell me have you forgotten
To give your throat a goodly spray
To keep the nasty bugs away?"

Wolf could hardly believe his ear;
Halitosis was his greatest fear.
So when at last the piggy said,
"I've got some spray to clear your head."
And passed it through the open window
And dropped it to the step below.
Wolfie gave his throat a squirt,
And suddenly it no longer hurt.
His breath became as sweet as roses,
Nice enough for any noses.
So since that day, I'm glad to say,
The wolf's bad breath has gone away,
And he and pig are best of mates,
Without a whiff of former hates.

Now if by chance you travel wide
You might just see them side by side,
Building houses of renown,
Instead of trying to blow them down.

Text Type: Poetic – Poem

Answers

Week 1

1 Doctor Humphries and patient (Mr Jones) **2** in the doctor's surgery **3** morning **4** to get test results back **5** Mr Jones has only one day to live. **6** The doctor should have told him yesterday. **7** yesterday **8** answers will vary, e.g. shock, horror **9** 0 **10** "Yes. I'm sorry," consoled the doctor. "One day left! If that's the good news, what's the bad news?" asked the patient. **11** see your teacher **12** see your teacher

Week 2

1 milking the cows **2** balanced the pail on her head **3** buy lots of eggs **4** She forgot about it and it slipped when she tossed her head. **5** Don't count your chickens before they hatch. **6** fantasies/dreams **7 a** chore **b** vanished **c** admire **d** chickens/poultry/fowls **e** profits **f** absorbed **g** buy **h** exactly

Week 3

1 KINGSFORD-SMITH AND ULM CROSS PACIFIC ... **2** SYDNEY TOWN LOW ON FOOD: COLONY MAY FAIL **3** NEW ROCK 'N' ROLL CRAZE SWEEPS ACROSS COUNTRY **4** STRANGE PAINTINGS FOUND IN CAVE BY THREE BOYS ... **5** *TITANIC* SINKS IN ATLANTIC: ICEBERG CLAIMS MANY VICTIMS **6** It was driven by an engine. **7** Her forces were defeated by the Romans. **8** ice **9** Brisbane **10** exploring

Week 4

1 self-raising **2** ¾ cup **3** butter, milk, cheese **4** to remove the lumps **5** salt **6** rubbed in with tips of fingers **7** add more milk **8** rolling pin **9** large pizza tray **10** ham, pineapple **11** Step 6 **12** so it is at the right temperature when you place the pizza in the oven **13** C = Centigrade, F = Fahrenheit **14** see your teacher **15 a** knead **b** chopped **c** required **d** brush **e** grated **f** bake

Week 5

Across: **3** burrow **4** milk **8** Australia **10** mammal **11** echidna **12** pouch **14** monotreme

Down: **1** quills **2** long **5** anteater **6** platypus **7** warm **8** amphibian **9** venom **13** spur

Week 6

1 true **2** true **3** false **4** true **5** false **6** false **7** true **8** false **9** see your teacher **10** see your teacher

Week 7

1 3 **2** 'Koala's in the Cradle', 'Twinkle, Twinkle Southern Cross' **3** Uluru Band, The Kelly Gang, The Rockaroos **4** 6 **5** 'A Touch of Surfers Paradise' **6** decreased: 'A Touch of Surfers Paradise', 'Gumbush', 'Let Me Be Your Koala Bear', 'Surfin' in the Bells Beach Classic', 'Puff the Magic Possum', 'Roll over Grant Hackett', 'She'll Be Comin' Round the Snowy Mountains'; increased: 'Bridge over Sydney Harbour', 'Give Me a Home on the Gold Coast', 'Crocodile Dundee Rock', 'Jumpin' Jack Kangaroo', 'Blue Suede Thongs', 'Click Go the Bails', 'Rock Around Uluru', 'Walk Like an Emu' **7** Australiana theme **8** answers will vary, e.g. 'Give Me a Home on the Gold Coast'; 'Surfin' in the Bells Beach Classic' **9** The Sydney Harbour Bridge is referred to as 'The Coathanger'. **10** answers will vary, e.g. 'Bridge over Troubled Waters', 'Click Go the Shears', 'Roll over Beethoven'

Week 8

1 Brentwood **2** hamburgers **3** unhealthy **4** slim/thin/trim **5** yoghurt **6** Oceanburger **7** seafood/fish **8** bones **9** Jumboburger **10** big **11** mouth **12** Kiddieburger **13** raspberry **14** hundreds **15** right **16** adults **17** fries **18** burnt **19** take **20** lives

Week 9

3, 7, 8, 1, 9, 10, 5, 4, 2, 6 **1** so that the sauce or pie will not drop onto you **2** to see if the filling is firm or runny **3** to cool it **4** to make it a nicer colour and to make it taste better **5** to clean any bits of pie and/or sauce off

Week 10

1 Jack **2** Castlemaine **3** surrender **4** Macoboy **5** sixteen **6** troopers **7** Beechworth **8** Davis **9** bushranger **10** Kelly

Week 11

1 6 **2** 300 – Eureka Tower; 270 – MIM Chimney; 5.9 – White pointer shark; 64 – CSIRO Radio Telescope; 2 739 000 – Darling River; 2228 – Mt Kosciuszko; 12 390 000 – National Highway; 335 – Uluru **3 a** Victoria **b** Queensland **c** NSW **d** Queensland **4 a** Queensland **b** Victoria **c** Northern Territory **d** NSW **e** NSW **f** ACT **g** NSW **h** Victoria

Week 12

1 ground **2** wife **3** brushes **4** coins **5** wealthy **6** old **7** jar **8** working **9** dead **10** pieces **11** answers will vary, e.g. found, discovered, had **12** answers will vary, e.g. throw in something else

Week 13

1 a BMX rally **b** maths **c** trivia afternoon **d** snail races **e** international news **f** baby photo competition **2** Mr Brown **3** ones from around the world **4** 12 **5** 'The Terminator' **6** 50 house points and a certificate **7** identify the most babies **8** 30 **9** answers will vary **10** 1 6 3 5 2 4

Week 14

see your teacher

Week 15

all answers will vary; examples follow:
1 At which city was the Olympic flag first raised? **2** In which year were the Olympic Games held in Amsterdam, Holland? **3** Who won eight gold medals for swimming at the Beijing Games? **4** Where were the Olympic Games first held in 1896? **5** How many gold medals did Larissa Latynina win? **6** Where will the Olympic Games be held in the year 2012? **7** Over how many years did Raimondo D'Inzeo compete to win his six gold medals?
8 see your teacher

Week 16

Jarvis; Kelly; 41; married; 3; taxation consultant; theatre, sport, spending time with family

Murray; Elisha; 39; married; 2; journalist; environment, sport

Owen; Deiniol; 37; married; 3; teacher; football, tennis, golf

1 Kelly Jarvis **2** Elisha Murray **3** Deiniol Owen **4** Elisha Murray **5** Elisha Murray **6** Kelly Jarvis **7** Elisha Murray **8** Kelly Jarvis **9** Deiniol Owen **10** Kelly Jarvis **11** Deiniol Owen **12** Elisha Murray

Week 17

1 along **2** pot **3** brick **4** spray **5** throat **6** friend **7** sweet **8** away **9** home **10** rotten

Week 18

Robot Attack; $49.95; computer; Compugame

1 trial **2** secret **3** disabled **4** lawyer **5** smart/ quick **6** fuzzy **7** level **8** groups

Week 19

6, 4, 8, 5, 3, 1, 2, 7; Cleaner; Second Doctor; Patient; Last Nurse

Week 20

Match up: 1 White light is made up of many colours. **2** Red flowers reflect red light. **3** Orange flowers reflect orange light. **4** Black things absorb all the colours. **5** All colours have different light waves. **6** Coloured lights change some colours. **Colour up:** the word is 'colour'

Week 21

Monday: Lunch at picnic ground; Stop at Dog on the Tucker Box; night walk; **Tuesday:** High Court; National Gallery; Regatta Point Planning Centre; Institute of Sport; indoor games; movie (*Get Smart*); ready for bed; **Wednesday:** breakfast; Electoral Office; lunch – Cockington Green; Parliament House; War Memorial; dinner; Telstra Tower; lights out; **Thursday:** Royal Mint; Questacon; lunch – Botanic Gardens; dinner; disco; ready for bed; lights out

Week 22

1 True **2** False **3** False **4** True **5** True **6** False **7** False **8** False **9** True **10** False

Week 23

1 Headhunter 3 **2** when they get a 'no' answer **3** pick category of choice **4** answers will vary, e.g. ask another question **5** 120 **6** 60 **7** Judy **8** Judy **9** David, Michael, Julie **10** see your teacher **11** 100 **12** 12 **13** 3 **14** *Mona Lisa*, *The Last Supper* **15** Johnny O'Keefe **16 a** literature **b** sport **c** yesteryear **d** film and television **e** music **f** literature

Week 24

1 Danger, Response, Airways, Breathing, Circulation **2** answers will vary, e.g. fire, electric wires, traffic **3** speak to them or shake them gently **4** turn patient onto side **5** to prevent air escaping **6** Their chest will rise. **7** adult – 15; child – 20 **8** Seek medical help immediately. **9** to clear the airways **10** the rise and fall of the chest

Week 25

1 10 **2** Jupiter **3** place of birth **4** female **5** no less than 10 000 galmarks **6** Australia **7** the magnetic stripe **8** within 48 hours (2 days) **9** The President-General of Australia **10** code of issuer **11** to a detention satellite **12** 3 July 2449

Week 26

see your teacher

Week 27

1 You will get sunburnt. **2** no; people who paste advertising posters onto walls **3** It has only three legs, it is mangy, has a broken tail and it is lost. **4** a date to meet someone **5** Dracula has fangs with which he bites people on the neck. **6** Mary gave birth to a little lamb; Humans don't give birth to lambs. **7** Kevin **8** a dried fruit **9** one under par scores in golf **10** The person did not like Steve. **11** faults in the Earth's crust **12** F

Week 28

Website: Discuss answers with your teacher and classmates. **Round up: Nouns** – head, coat, cattle, Kelpies; **Verbs** – bred, herd, train, nip; **Adjectives** – hardworking, wild, firm, fearless; **Adverbs** – safely, gently, quietly, finally

Week 29

1 Aries **2** Taurus **3** Cancer **4** Scorpio **5** Aquarius **6** Capricorn **7** Sagittarius **8** Virgo **9** yes; Capricorn (not a thing will happen) **10** answers will vary, e.g. might, could, possibility **11** cerise, carmine, scarlet **12** ochre, umber, sepia **13** see your teacher

Week 30

1 Life on the goldfields is very difficult. **2** answers will vary, e.g. the weather; food was scarce and expensive; hard work **3** He had to purchase equipment that was very expensive. **4** finding gold **5** not used to hard work **6** as tough as leather; as old as the hills; as cold as ice; as hungry as a horse; as black as coal; as flat as a tack; as keen as mustard **7** cost; constant inspections **8 a** purchasing **b** gambled **c** constant **d** expensive **e** harsh **f** abandon

Week 31

answers will vary; examples follow: **1** Where did the subject put the piece of paper? **2** Which Chinese restaurant did the subject eat in? **3** How far is it from the subject's house to McDuck's restaurant? **4** Where was the car waiting for the subject? **5** Who did the subject pass his rail ticket to? **6** Why did the subject buy three tickets for the movie theatre? **7** What did Agent Sharp do to his shoe to stop himself feeling hungry? **8** When did Agent Sharp realise that the subject had left the movie theatre? **9** Why did Agent Sharp leave Agent Cuckoo behind? **10** Where did the subject buy the newspaper?

Week 32

1 nine **2** left-hand side **3** Wrap the wire around the paper fastener. **4 a** 2 **b** 2 **5** A circuit is formed. **6** Nothing – no circuit is formed. **7** see your teacher **8** Death by electrocution can result. **9** New South Wales – Sydney; Tasmania – Hobart; Victoria – Melbourne; Queensland – Brisbane; Western Australia – Perth; South Australia – Adelaide; Northern Territory – Darwin

Week 33

1 suit **2** kids (children) **3** face **4** look **5** sauce **6** luck **7** road **8** mates **9** hearts **10** corner **11** chance **12** boot **13** eye **14** pie **15** town **16** fingers **17** feet **18** lies **19** pocket **20** cold **21** thief **22** jewellery **23** arms

Week 34

1 finished last **2** Entreaty; Nightraid **3** two **4** express train **5** Red Terror; Lightning **6** No. See your teacher for reason. **7** The past four Melbourne Cup winners had seven letters in their names. **8** because of his breeding (related to Carbine on both sides) **9** He will win a Melbourne Cup. **10** see your teacher

Week 35

1 48 **2** 8 **3** external skeleton **4** they have oil on their legs **5** begins outside the body **6** difference in the number of species of spiders **7** see your teacher **8** arachnophobia **a** closed spaces **b** water **c** heights **d** germs **e** animals **f** fears

9

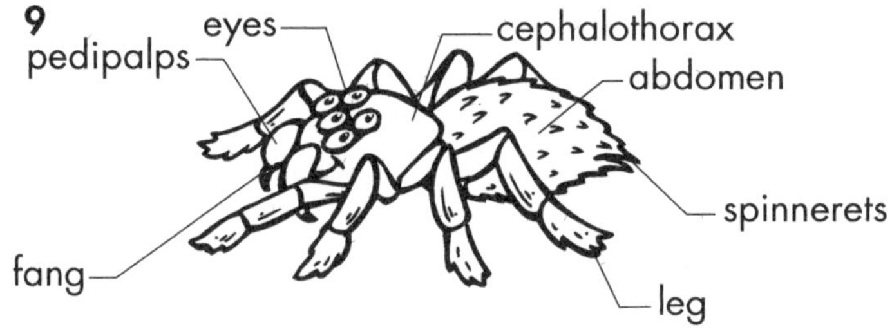

10 see your teacher

Complete each of these verses:

1. As you know in verse and song,
   Wolves and pigs don't get ____________________
2. You must remember the wolf did not
   End up in the piggie's ____________________
3. The wolf nearly made himself sick,
   Huffing and puffing at the house of ____________________
4. The very thing that saved the day,
   Was when the pig threw down a tin of ____________________
5. To help his breath you must note,
   The wolf just had to spray his ____________________
6. The thing that's pleasing to the end,
   Is that the wolf found a pig for a ____________________
7. No matter who the wolf does meet,
   His breath will smell so very ____________________
8. Since the pig gave the wolf his spray,
   The wolf's bad breath has gone ____________________
9. Now the two are known to roam,
   Building, instead of destroying a ____________________
10. Just in case you have forgotten,
    The wolf's breath was really ____________________

Moving on

You might have noticed that this poem was made up of rhyming couplets. This means that each pair of lines rhymes. Use this style to write a poem about some other fairytale characters.

Robot Attack

Computer Game Review

Reviewed by I.Q. JONES

Game: Robot Attack

Robot Attack is from the Compugame range and is priced at a reasonable $49.95. Players must try to resist the invasion of Earth by robots who have been created by the mad scientist Dr Gargon, who was exiled to the Planet Zell.

To advance through the first level, players must try to find out where the scientist is sending his instructions from. This means finding the secret location of his laboratory somewhere on the Planet Zell.

The player must then recruit a team of smart friends who have the brains to work out how to upset the computerised machinery that operates the robots. The robots are organised into groups that must be isolated and put out of action before the robot chief can be tackled. This is achieved only with a great deal of figuring out and cunning moves.

The final stage is locating Dr Gargon and escorting him back to Earth for trial before the Interplanetary Court. And here is the interesting part. The player must try to prove the charges against the doctor, who is defended by a very smart lawyer.

The graphics used in this game are very good. The control panels are just like the real thing with a large number of whizz-bang effects. There is a little fuzziness about the sound, but it is mostly in keeping with the action on the screen. This is a very challenging game where the player must not only be quick with the controls, but must also do a lot of thinking.

This is one of the best computer games around and can keep the player entertained for hours on end. At $49.95 it is great value for money.

Graphics: 85%
Sound: 80%
Challenge Value: 95%
Entertainment Value: 90%
Value for Money: 100%

Text Type: Exposition – Review

Complete the table of information.

Name of Game	
Price	
Type of Game	
Manufacturer	

Circle the word that best completes each sentence.

1. Players must try to send Dr Gargon back to Earth for
   instructions trial charges action
2. The laboratory on Planet Zell is
   secret underground destroyed fuzzy
3. Before trying to catch the robot chief, the robots must be
   created disabled defended recruited
4. To send Dr Gargon to gaol you must out-think his
   robots brains friends lawyer
5. To win the game players must be
   young smart quick isolated
6. The sound for this game is
   fuzzy whizz-bang challenging value
7. You need to find where the instructions are coming from to get through the first
   planet secret computer level
8. The robots are organised into
   laboratories groups graphics levels

Moving on

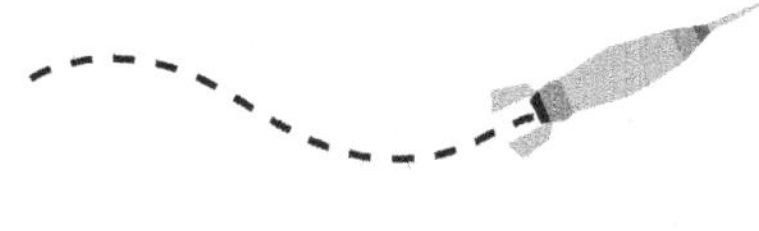

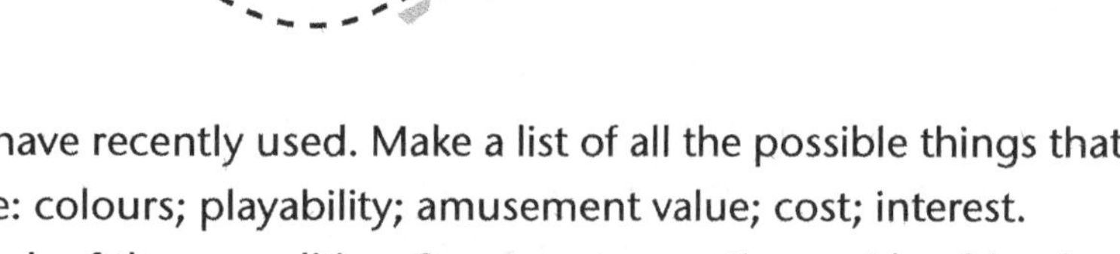

Start with a game or toy that you have recently used. Make a list of all the possible things that you could judge it on, for example: colours; playability; amusement value; cost; interest. Next, create some way of rating each of these qualities. Compare your ratings with a friend.

The Operation – A One-act Play

Cast	First Doctor, Second Doctor, Head Nurse, five other Nurses, two Cleaners, Tea-person, Patient
Scene	*An operating theatre. The Patient is on the table, covered by a sheet which reaches to the floor. The Nurses are standing around chatting and reading magazines. Doctors enter, Second Doctor with golf bag slung over shoulder.*
Second Doctor:	Well, what's on today?
First Doctor:	A pestasectomy.
Second Doctor:	Well, let's get started. I've got to be on the golf course by ten.
First Doctor:	(*Issues order to Second Doctor*) Hammer … er … I mean anaesthetic.
Second Doctor:	(*Turns and issues order to Head Nurse)* Anaesthetic.
Head Nurse:	(*Turns and issues order to next Nurse*) Anaesthetic. (*This is repeated down the line until the last Nurse, who turns to nobody and repeats the order. The Last Nurse laughs and picks up a hammer, which is passed down the line to the First Doctor. A good thump on the table puts the patient out.*)
First Doctor:	(*Issues order to Second Doctor*) Scalpel. (*This is repeated as before. The Last Nurse realises no one is there and laughs. A large carving knife is passed down the line.*)
Second Doctor:	Ouch! (*As the Head Nurse passes the knife – blade first!*)
First Doctor:	(*First doctor proceeds to cut open the patient with exaggerated actions.*) Well, what have we here? (*Proceeds to pull out an old boot, which is handed up by a person under the table; a string of sausages, which he tosses in the direction of the Nurses, who all scream; and finally an alarm clock, which is ringing.*)
	Enter: Cleaners, sweeping dust everywhere
Cleaners:	Excuse us. Coming through. Just carry on. (*Doctors, Nurses and Patient all begin to cough.*)
First Doctor:	Well let's sew him up. Needle and thread. (*This is repeated as before and a very large needle and string are passed back.*) I can never thread this stupid thing. Here, you do it. (*This is repeated as before.*)
Last Nurse:	(*Turning to no one*) Here, you do it. (*Laughs*) Silly me. Oh, very well, I'll do it. (*Needle and thread are passed down the line and First Doctor begins sewing up patient with exaggerated gestures.*)
	Enter: Tea-person pushing trolley
Tea-person:	Coffee, tea or hot chocolate? (*Doctors and Nurses rush over and begin having some drinks. Patient begins to get up. Doctor walks over and pushes Patient back down. Finish drinks and return. Finish sewing up Patient.*)
Second Doctor:	Well, that's that. (*Patient gets up of own accord.*) Now off to the golf course. What's the time?
First Doctor:	My watch! Where's my watch? Hey you. Come back here.
Patient:	Not on your life! (*Flees off stage, chased by Doctors and Nurses.*)

● **Text Type:** Narrative – Play

Put these phrases in the order in which they occurred in the play. Place a '1' next to the phrase that comes first, a '2' beside the one that comes next, and so on.

______ Everyone starts coughing

______ Doctor removes the old boot

______ Doctors and Nurses chase patient

______ Nurses scream

______ Doctor issues order for a scalpel

______ Nurses reading magazines

______ Patient hit on the head

______ Doctor drinks a cup of tea

Below are four thought clouds. Draw and label which actor would have thought each of these during the play. The first one has been done for you.

Moving on

Perform the play. Assign roles, practise, organise costumes and then perform the play to an audience.

What Is Colour?

The colours red, orange, yellow, green, blue, indigo and violet make up the colours of the spectrum. When mixed together they produce white light. You can see these colours when you see a rainbow. The drops of water in a rainy sky break the sunlight into the different colours.

Things that have colour do something special. When white light shines on them, they absorb (swallow up) some of the colours in the light and reflect (shine back) the other colours in the light. A red flower absorbs the other colours and reflects the red colour. An orange flower absorbs the other colours and reflects the orange colour.

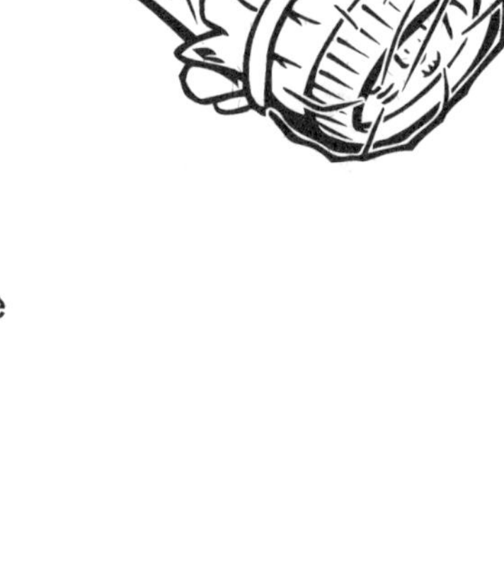

White things reflect all the light, so they look white. Black things absorb all the light, so they don't reflect any colour at all.

The colour of something can change when you shine a coloured light on it. You could try shining a red light on something to see if its colour changes. Then try a blue light, and so on. Just wrap differently coloured pieces of cellophane over a torch and see what happens.

Our eyes see these colours because each colour has its own special light wave. Some are longer waves that travel slowly, and others are shorter waves that travel more quickly. Our brains work out what the colours should be. Most people can see all the colours.

Text Type: Information - Scientific Facts

Match up

Match up the parts of the sentences to make them true statements.

White light	absorb	different light waves.
Red flowers	change	all the colours.
Orange flowers	is made up	some colours.
Black things	reflect	of many colours.
All colours	have	orange light.
Coloured lights	reflect	red light.

1. ______________________________
2. ______________________________
3. ______________________________
4. ______________________________
5. ______________________________
6. ______________________________

Colour up

Colour in the picture using the colour key and find a message in the picture.

BK = black R = red B = blue G = green Y = yellow
P = purple O = orange PK = pink BR = brown

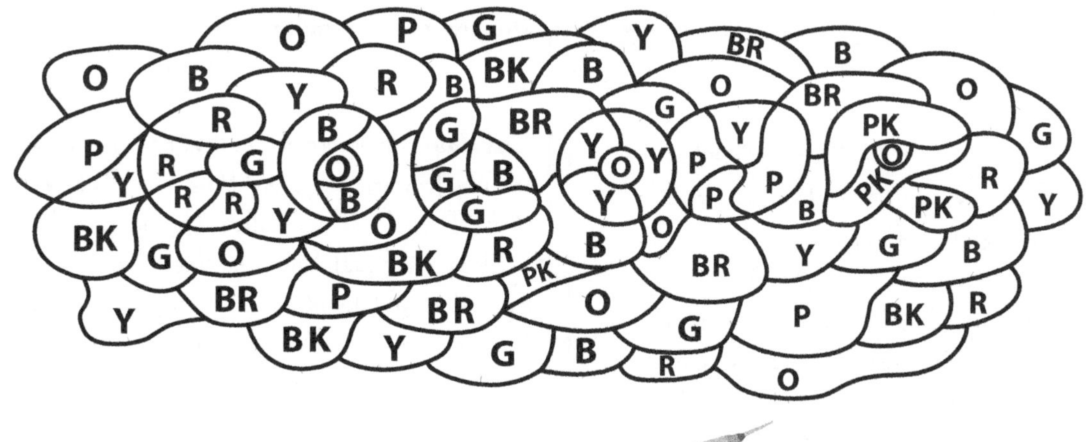

Moving on

Put a coloured piece of cellophane over a torch and shine it on something. What happens to the colour of the thing you shine the torch on? Do it again using pieces of cellophane of different colours. What happens?

Camp Diary

Grade 6 went on a five-day trip to Canberra. They were asked to keep a diary in their camp booklets. Here are the instructions given to the students on what to write about in their diaries, as well as Belinda's diary entries.

Imagine if someone said to you, "What did you do in Canberra?" Would you remember everything? Keep a diary of the events that happened during the week. Make your diary a good piece of writing.

Monday, 30 November

(Include something of the bus trip, the weather, your impressions of Canberra and the night walk.)

Waved goodbye to Mum and we were off on our way to Canberra. Mum was crying but I was really excited. It was raining when we left but it had stopped by the time we got to Shepparton. The bus trip seemed to take forever but it wasn't too bad – we had movies and the bus driver is really cool. We had lunch at a picnic ground and then stopped at the Dog on the Tucker Box (can't remember the name of the place). We got to Canberra about 6 o'clock and then had dinner. (Yuk! I'll never complain about Mum's cooking again.) We went for a night walk and Mr Brown got us lost. We are going to have a midnight snack. Bye.

Tuesday, 1 December

(Mention the many places we visited as well as something about the Indoor Games evening.)

Boy am I tired. We didn't go to sleep until 3 o'clock. We had a really busy day. This morning we went to the National Library (boring), The High Court (interesting) and the National Gallery. We then went to the Regatta Point Planning Centre and saw a movie. We had lunch next to Lake Burley Griffin. In the afternoon we went to the Institute of Sport – it was great. We saw Tamsin Lewis. The meals are really gross (lunch is the only good meal). Tonight we are having indoor games and a movie – Get Smart (I've seen it). Bye.

P.S. The indoor games were cool.

Wednesday, 2 December

(What was your impression of Parliament House? Also write about the night visit to the Telstra Tower.)

Stayed up late talking. So tired! Breakfast was yuk – sloppy spaghetti. This morning we went to the Electoral Office and had an election. Then we went on a tour of the embassies. We had lunch at Cockington Green – a miniature village. After lunch we went to Parliament House and had a mini-parliament. We went to the War Memorial before dinner – that was okay. Don the bus driver is crazy. It felt like he went around a big roundabout 13 times. Can you believe it? Tonight we are going to Telstra Tower.

See ya.

Thursday, 3 December

(Write about your visit to Questacon, your free afternoon and tonight's disco.)

Last day. Tomorrow we go home. I guess I'm looking forward to seeing Mum and Dad but DEFINITELY not my sister! This morning we went to the Royal Mint and then Questacon. It was great. All hands-on. We spent three hours there and didn't want to leave. We had lunch at the Botanic Gardens and then went back to the Heritage Centre (our home). We had a free afternoon and some kids went shopping but I stayed back and swam in the pool. Don was crazy as usual. Really looking forward to the disco tonight. Tell you about that tomorrow. Bye.

Text Type: Recount – Diary

Below is the timetabled itinerary for the Grade 6 trip to Canberra. It appeared in the camp booklet, but it is only partially completed. By referring to Belinda's camp diary, can you complete the itinerary?

ITINERARY

Monday, 30 November

7:45 a.m.	Assemble at school
8:00 a.m.	Depart school
10:30 a.m.	Arrive Shepparton – toilet break
12:30 a.m.	
3:00 p.m.	
5:45 p.m.	Short tour of Canberra
6:15 p.m.	Settle in at the Heritage Centre
6:45 p.m.	Dinner
8:00 p.m.	
10:30 p.m.	Ready for bed
11:00 p.m.	Lights out (sleep tight)

Tuesday, 1 December

7:30 a.m.	Breakfast
9:00 a.m.	National Library
9:45 a.m.	
10:30 a.m.	
11:45 a.m.	
12:30 p.m.	Lunch next to Lake Burley Griffin
2:00 p.m.	
6:30 p.m.	Dinner
7:30 p.m.	
8:30 p.m.	
10:30 p.m.	
11:00 p.m.	Lights out (and GO TO SLEEP!)

Wednesday, 2 December

7:30 a.m.	
9:00 a.m.	
11:00 a.m.	Tour of the embassies
12:30 p.m.	
2:00 p.m.	
4:30 p.m.	
6:30 p.m.	
7:15 p.m.	Foot rally – scavenger hunt
8:00 p.m.	
10:00 p.m.	Ready for bed
10:30 p.m.	

Thursday, 3 December

7:30 a.m.	Breakfast
9:00 a.m.	
9:30 a.m.	
12:30 p.m.	
2:00 p.m.	Free afternoon – shopping, swim in the pool or visit the Film and Sound Archives
5:00 p.m.	Staff-versus-students softball match
6:30 p.m.	
8:00 p.m.	
10:30 p.m.	
11:00 p.m.	

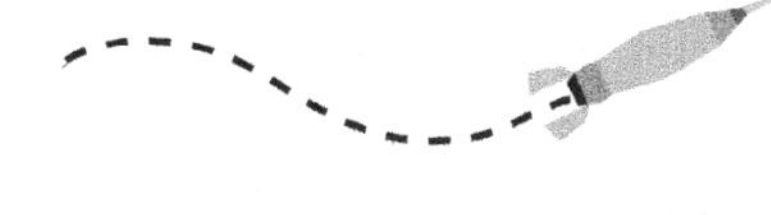

Plan an itinerary for a week's holiday to anywhere you wish. Some travel brochures might be useful to help you do this.

A Roo Called Fred

Aunty Mug loved horses too much to be a successful trainer. She was too attached to them. Any horses, from old Sampson who was nearly thirty now and who'd pulled a plough before the war, to the Golden Queen who'd won the Geelong Cup twenty years ago and still grazed the lower paddock. There were other horses too, winners from old races and ones who'd never won at all. Aunty Mug had bred them all, and loved them.

"Where's Fred?" asked Bernie, looking around.

Mug put her fingers to her mouth and whistled. The noise echoed round the courtyard and sheds and yards. There was a thumping outside the shed and Fred bounded out. He was taller than Aunty Mug now, and almost twice as wide, a giant of an eastern grey. His back was dusty where he'd been lying in the sun. He came up behind Aunty Mug and put his furry arms around her neck.

"Aaaagh," he said as he held his head down and scratched.

"Get off," said Aunty Mug. "Come on, you great galoot. You tickle. Come round in front."

Like Harold, Fred had come down to Redgate Farm as an almost hairless baby after shooters got his mother. He was fully grown now, but still loped around the farm, sampling horse tucker and jumping at the geese.

"I bet he's the biggest roo around," said Annabelle proudly as she scratched his ears.

"He eats enough." said Aunty Mug. "No-one'd believe now how tiny he was when those shooters brought him in. I never thought I'd raise him, not all bald as a rat as he was. No, get your nose out of my pocket, Fred. There's no tucker for you there. You're old enough to get your own food."

"Could I get him some bread? Please Aunty Mug?"

"There's some stale in the top of the bread bin," said Aunty Mug. "You're spoilt, Fred. That's your trouble."

"Aaaagh," said Fred. He leant back on his tail and lifted one leg playfully. Aunty Mug pushed it back down. "None of that," she said. "You're too big, Fred. You can hurt someone like that." She shook her head. "You've got to be careful with boy roos. I had one rip up a dog of mine once. That was the last dog I ever had. The roo was Roger. He was big, but not as big as Fred. I said then I would never have another boy roo, they get too stroppy, I'll stick to the girls. But I couldn't refuse Fred when they brought him in. No bigger than a skinned rabbit, were you Fred, and eyes like a baby possum's."

Ten-horse race

There are ten horses in this race. To find out where your horse finishes in the race, select the true or false answer for each statement. If you get ten correct, you come first; if you get nine correct, you come second; eight correct wins you third place, etc.

START

FINISH

1 Aunty Mug was shorter than Fred.
T F

2 Golden Queen had won the Melbourne Cup.
T F

3 Fred had been shot by hunters.
T F

4 Fred loved horse feed.
T F

5 Male kangaroos can be dangerous.
T F

6 Aunty Mug fed Fred stale bread from her pocket.
T F

7 Female kangaroos are twice as wide as the males.
T F

8 The sun had made Fred's back dusty.
T F

9 Aunty Mug loved spoiling Fred.
T F

10 Baby Fred was smaller than a skinned rabbit.
T F

Moving on

Use the Internet to find out the last five winners (horses and jockeys) of the Melbourne Cup.

Week 23

Headhunt

A game for 2 to 6 people

Age: 9 to adult

Aim: To be the first 'headhunter' to discover their identity through Yes and No questioning

Contents:

- **6 headbands**
- **500 cards (divided into five categories)**
- **1 category die**
- **1 score card**

	Round				
Headhunter	**1**	**2**	**3**	**4**	**Total**
1 David	80	60	100	80	320
2 Melissa	120	100	60	20	300
3 Katie	60	80	40	120	300
4 Michael	100	20	20	60	200
5 Judy	40	120	120	100	380
6 Julie	20	40	80	40	180

Rules

- Headhunter 1 rolls the category die, draws the top card from that pile and places the card in the headband of Headhunter 2, making sure Headhunter 2 does not see the card. This is repeated until every headhunter has a card.
- Headhunters take it in turns asking questions that can only be answered with a Yes or No answer to try to determine the identity displayed on the card in their headband. A Yes answer entitles the headhunter to ask another question. A No answer results in the loss of a turn.

Scoring

The first headhunter to discover their identity scores 120 points, the second headhunter to discover their identity scores 100 points, the third scores 80 points ... down to 20 points for the sixth headhunter (see score card above).

Cards

Here are six of the 'Headhunt' cards from various categories (brief information on each identity is provided on each card).

James Bond (007)
Secret service character created by Ian Fleming (1908–1964) in his first book ***Casino Royale***. All of his 12 books have been made into successful movies.

Dawn Fraser (1937–)
Australian swimmer. Won the same Olympic title – the 100-metres freestyle – at three successive Games: 1956, 1960 and 1964. Received a 10-year ban when she souvenired a flag from the Emperor's Tokyo palace.

Leonardo da Vinci (1452–1519)
Italian artist and scientific genius who was years ahead of his contemporaries. Painted the ***Mona Lisa*** and ***The Last Supper***. Wrote 5000 pages of notes – all in mirror writing.

Groucho Marx (1890–1977)
With his brothers, Harpo and Chico, made many comedy movies including ***A Night at the Opera***. Always joking, he said, "I don't mind dying – I just don't want to be there when it happens."

Johnny O'Keefe (1935–1978)
Known as the 'Wild One', O'Keefe was recognised as Australia's King of Rock 'n' Roll with hits such as 'Shout' and 'She Wears My Ring'. Compered Australia's first rock 'n' roll TV show, ***Six O'Clock Rock***.

Aladdin
One of a collection of 200 stories that make up the famous piece of Arabic literature, ***The Arabian Nights***, also known as ***The Thousand and One Nights***, written during the 1500s.

Text Type: Information / Procedural – Game

The rules

1. On whose headband would Headhunter 2 place a category card? ____________
2. When does a headhunter's turn end? ____________
3. What do you think happens if the die lands on 'Free Choice'? ____________
4. What would you suggest happens if the headhunters don't know the answer to a Yes/No question? ____________

The scoring/scorecard

5. How many points does the winner of a round score? ____________
6. If you are the fourth person to discover your identity, how many points do you get? ______
7. Who won the game shown on the score card? ____________
8. Who won the most rounds? ____________
9. Which players didn't win a round? ____________
10. Do you think this is a good method of scoring? Give a reason for your answer. ____________

The category cards

11. How many cards are there in each category? ____________
12. How many James Bond books did Ian Fleming write? ____________
13. How many Olympic gold medals did Dawn Fraser win in the 100-metres freestyle? ______
14. Name two paintings by Leonardo da Vinci. ____________ ____________
15. Who compered Australia's first rock 'n' roll television show? ____________
16. Write which category each of the six cards shown belongs to: Sport; Yesteryear; Literature; Music; Film and TV.

a James Bond ____________ **b** Dawn Fraser ____________

c Leonardo da Vinci ____________ **d** Groucho Marx ____________

e Johnny O'Keefe ____________ **f** Aladdin ____________

Write down three identities for each category. Play a game of Headhunt. You can improvise by writing the name of a well-known identity on a sticky note and placing this on the hat of another headhunter.

In an Emergency

Accidents can happen at any time – at home, at school, in the bush. Would you know what to do if a friend suffered an accident or serious illness? In an emergency, follow the DRABC Action Plan. Study the DRABC chart below.

1 D is for Danger

- Always check for any danger to yourself, others and the patient.
- Only continue if it is safe to do so.

2 R is for Response

- Check if the patient is conscious. Do this by speaking to them or shaking them gently.
- If there is a response, treat other injuries.
- If there is no response, proceed with 'Airways'.

3 A is for Airways

- Turn patient onto side facing away from you, making sure you support the neck.
- Tilt the head back gently.
- Open the mouth. Clear anything obstructing the airway.

4 B is for Breathing

- Check the breathing by listening and looking at chest.
- If patient is breathing, leave patient on side and treat other injuries.
- If patient is not breathing, begin Expired Air Resuscitation (Mouth-to-Mouth).

Expired Air Resuscitation

- Gently turn the patient onto their back and tilt their head back. Use a pistol grip to support the jaw and open the mouth.
- Breathe deeply into patient's mouth to inflate lungs. Pinch nose to prevent air escaping. Give five short breaths. *Note*: For a small child or baby, give small puffs of air from your cheeks, covering both the nose and the mouth with your mouth.
- Watch for the fall and rise of the chest between breaths.

5 C is for Circulation

- Check pulse.
- If pulse is present, continue Mouth-to-Mouth (15 a minute, 20 a minute for children) until normal breathing returns.
- If there is no pulse, begin Cardiopulmonary Resuscitation (CPR) BUT only if you are trained to do so. If not, seek medical help immediately.

Text Type: Procedural – Instructions

The DRABC Action Plan

1. The Action Plan is sometimes referred to as the Doctor ABC Plan. Write what each letter of the plan stands for. ______________________

2. List three different situations that could pose a danger to yourself when aiding a casualty.

3. How do you check to see if a patient is conscious?

4. If a patient is unconscious, what is the first thing you do?

5. Why do you pinch the patient's nose during Expired Air Resuscitation?

6. How do you know you have successfully inflated the patient's lungs?

7. How many breaths a minute must you give when applying Expired Air Resuscitation?
   For an adult: ____________ For a child: ____________

8. If there is no pulse and you are untrained in Cardiopulmonary Resuscitation (CPR), what must you do? ____________

9. Why would you turn the patient onto their side if there is no response?

10. What would tell you that air has moved in and out of the patient's lungs?

Moving on

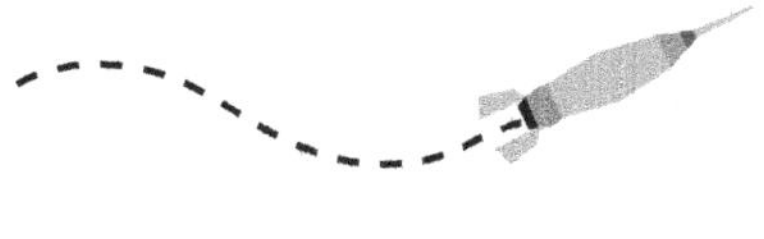

Find out about and write down the procedures for Cardiopulmonary Resuscitation (CPR).

Spaceport Passport

In order to travel to Spaceport Delphi in the fourth precinct of Mars orbit, a special passport should be carried at all times, a sample of which is reproduced below.

SPACE PASSPORT

THE BEARER SHOULD BE AWARE THAT THIS PASSPORT IS NOT VALID FOR REGIONS BEYOND JUPITER, AND THAT ANY PERSON WITHOUT A PROPER PASSPORT IN REGIONS BEYOND JUPITER MAY ATTRACT A FINE OF NO LESS THAN 10 000 GALMARKS AND WILL HAVE TO SURRENDER THIS PASSPORT TO THE GALACTIC POLICE. GALACTIC PASSPORT HOLDERS WHO LOSE THEIR PASSPORTS MUST NOTIFY THEIR NEAREST GALACTIC POLICE STATION WITHIN 48 EARTH HOURS. FAILURE TO DO SO MAY RESULT IN THE OFFENDER BEING CONFINED TO THE NEAREST DETENTION SATELLITE.

REGION ISSUING PASSPORT: Australia PASSPORT NO.: SP326-769024
REGAS PASPOR ISSENT PASPOR NO.

CODE OF ISSUER: AUS TYPE: SP
ISSENTOR CODA TYPA

SURNAME: Clark
SURNOM

GIVEN NAMES: Tula Stellar
NOMS A LOT

NATIONALITY: Australian
NASONALI

SEX: F PLACE OF BIRTH: Genopolis, AUS
SEX GENA PIAS

DATE OF ISSUE: 3 JUL 2439 DATE OF EXPIRY: 3 JUL 2449
ISSENT DATA EXPIR DATA

HOLDER'S SIGNATURE *TS Clark*
SIGNA MANIS

THE PRESIDENT-GENERAL OF AUSTRALIA, BEING THE REPRESENTATIVE OF THE EARTH GOVERNMENT IN AUSTRALIA, REQUESTS THAT ALL TO WHOM THIS PASSPORT IS SHOWN WILL ALLOW THE BEARER TO PASS FREELY THROUGHOUT THE GALACTICAL REGION INDICATED WITHOUT INTERFERENCE AND TO GIVE EVERY ASSISTANCE TO THE BEARER AND PROVIDE ANY PROTECTION THAT MAY BE NEEDED.

OFFICERS CHECKING THIS PASSPORT SHOULD CHECK THE MAGNETIC STRIPE BELOW FOR FULL DETAILS OF THE BEARER'S PERSONAL AND PUBLIC ACTIVITIES.

- **Text Type:** Information – Passport

You are a member of the Galactic Police Force. You need to understand what appears on the Spaceport Passport.

1 The passport is good for how many years?

____

2 The passport is good only as far as which planet?

____

3 What is English for ***Gena pias***?

____

4 Is Tula Clark male or female?

____

5 What is the fine for anyone found not carrying a passport?

____

6 Which country has the person come from?

____

7 Where can the police check the person's personal details?

____

8 How long is the passport holder given to notify the Galactic Police if the passport is lost?

____

9 Who is the Earth Government's representative in Australia?

____

10 What does ***Issentor coda*** mean in English?

____

11 Where could people who break the rules be sent if they cannot show their passport?

____

12 On what date does this passport expire?

____

Moving on

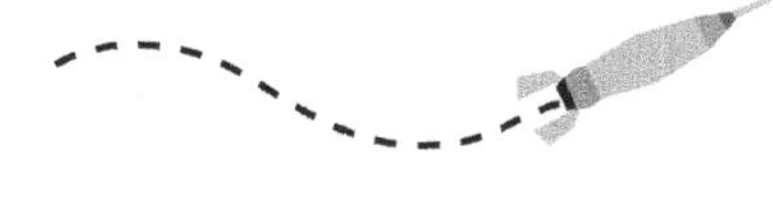

Make up a passport that will entitle the bearer to go to a special place, e.g. the centre of the Earth, the bottom of the sea or into a volcano.

The Giant Turnip

A poor soldier came back from the wars and found that his rich brother would have nothing to do with him. The rich brother even shut the door in his face.

So the soldier took off his uniform and turned farmer. He dug and hoed his bit of land and sowed it with turnip seed. The seed came up. One of the turnips was larger and stronger than the rest. It grew and grew, and seemed as if it would never stop growing. Never was such a turnip seen before and never will such a one be seen again.

At last it was so enormous it filled a cart and two oxen were required to pull it.

"This must be the King of Turnips!" said the soldier. "Whatever shall I do with it? No one will want to buy it, for small turnips taste better than large ones. I'd better take it to the King and make him a present of it."

The soldier took his turnip in a cart, drawn by two oxen, to the palace and presented it to the King.

"Well, well!" said the King, "I've seen many wonderful things but never, never have I seen such a monster as this turnip. How did you grow it? What is your secret?"

"I've no secret," said the soldier, "I planted turnip seed in the usual way and one turnip grew to this size."

"Then you must be a favourite of good fortune!" said the King.

"I am not," said the soldier, and he went on to tell the King how he had returned from the wars and how his brother had shut the door in his face.

"You shall be as rich as your brother," said the King, and he ordered gold and silver to be loaded onto the soldier's cart until it could hold no more. Altogether it was a fortune.

When the rich brother heard about this fortune his brother had gained with one turnip, he was filled with envy, and he wondered how he could add to his wealth by pleasing the King.

"My brother gave the King the best he had. If I do the same, he'll surely reward me with real treasure."

So he ordered his servants to load his best gold plates and his wife's richest jewels onto the backs of six of his finest horses, and rode with them to the palace.

The King said he was amazed at the splendour of the gifts, and that he'd like to show his appreciation of such generosity.

"You shall have the most wonderful thing I possess," said he. "This wonderful turnip!"

The rich brother had to accept the turnip – there was nothing else he could do. It was all he got in exchange for the gold and rich jewels he had given the King. And it was all he deserved.

A Traditional German Folk Tale

Text Type: Narrative – Traditional Tale

Retell the story *The Giant Turnip* in your own words by writing one or two sentences to match each picture.

Week 27

No Graffiti Here!

Philatelists should be stamped out!

Foo was here

Roses are red
Sunburn is too
So keep your shirt on!

what is the capital of Australia?

A

I'd like a date.

HOW ABOUT 1788

Roses are red
Daisies are yellow
I think that Kevin (that's me)
Is a really nice fellow.

where can I find another boy like Steve?

TRY THE ZOO! HA

Venus de Milo is armless.

Mary had a little lamb
And all the doctors fainted

NO GRAFFITI HERE!

DRACULA IS A PAIN IN THE NECK

Tiger Woods HITS BIRDIES

EATHQUAKES ARE NOBODY'S FAULT

LOST-three legged, one-eyed mangy dog with broken tail. Answers to the name of Lucky

I'd like a date.
Ring 73 412.

Sorry, I've only got a sultana.

BILL POSTERS WILL BE FINED

Bill Posters is innocent!

AUSSIES RULES OK!

Text Type: Exposition – Graffiti

Could you make sense of the graffiti?

1. This will happen to you if you do not slip on a shirt.
2. Is there such a person as Bill Posters?

   If not, what is, or are, bill posters?
3. What is unlucky about 'Lucky'?
4. What sort of date was the person writing that message referring to?
5. How is Dracula a 'pain in the neck'?
6. Why did the doctors faint?

   What was unusual about that?
7. Who thinks that Kevin is nice?
8. What sort of date did the second person joke about when mentioning the sultana?
9. What sort of birdies would Tiger Woods hit?
10. What did the second person think about Steve?
11. What sort of faults are earthquakes?
12. What would the capital of France be, according to the graffiti?

WARNING Writing graffiti is illegal in most places. The cleaning of graffiti costs our communities millions of dollars every year.

Moving on

Ask your teacher to set up a graffiti board in the room so that clever or funny (not nasty, rude or insulting) sayings can be put there as well as other comments that tell of your likes or dislikes.

Cattle Dogs of Australia

The Kelpie

PORTRAIT: The Kelpie has a strong, muscular body and well-developed legs. It stands 43 to 51 cm high and has a body mass of 11.5 to 20.5 kg. The Kelpie is slightly longer than it is high, has a broad chest and firm hindquarters. It has a dense undercoat of hair and a hard, water-repellent outer coat that is coloured either black, tan, fawn, chocolate or bluish.

DEVELOPMENT: Kelpies were bred from English North Country Collies of the Rutherford type, which were brought to Australia because they are such good sheep and cattle dogs with a natural instinct to herd these animals. In Australia, they have been used on farms to work cattle, sheep, goats, poultry and deer.

CHARACTER: Kelpies are faithful, one-person dogs. As farm dogs they are not suitable for confinement on small blocks of land. They are easy to train and are hardworking.

Australian Cattle Dog

Also known as Queensland or Blue Heeler

PORTRAIT: The Cattle Dog is noted for its strength. Its head is balanced with its body; its shoulders are broad and well developed; its chest is deep and muscular. It has a short, thick outer coat. The hair on its tail is long and thick enough to comb into a 'broom'. The Cattle Dog stands 43 to 48 cm at the top of the shoulders (withers) and has a body mass of 14 to 19 kg.

DEVELOPMENT: Australian cattle farmers needed a dog that would safely drive their cattle to market. Sixty years of cross-breeding with Bull Terriers, Dalmatians, Kelpies, wild Dingoes and Collies finally produced the Australian Cattle Dog.

CHARACTER: Cattle Dogs work quietly so as not to frighten the cattle. They nip gently at the cattle's legs to move them along. They can also herd horses, goats and even ducks with great skill. Cattle Dogs can be fierce when angry thanks to their Dingo ancestors. They are 100% working dogs; fearless and determined.

You are making a website about dogs. Fill in the details about these dogs for your site.

Kelpie	**Australian Cattle Dog**
Other names:	Other names:
Height:	Height:
Mass:	Mass:
Coat:	Coat:
Colours:	Colours:
Bred from:	Bred from:
Character:	Character:
Used for:	Used for:

Round up: Help the Cattle Dog herd these parts of speech into their correct pens.

head safely
bred hardworking
gently herd coat
train quietly
wild firm Kelpies
cattle nip
fearless finally

Nouns	**Verbs**

Adjectives	**Adverbs**

Use the model above to list details about a pet you own or would like to own.

Madame Guessalot's Starscope

Aquarius
21 Jan–19 Feb
Avoid any conflicts with brothers and sisters today. You'll come off second best, especially if they are bigger than you.
Lucky Number – 8
Lucky Colour – Magenta

Pisces
20 Feb–20 Mar
If you stand at your letterbox you might meet someone new. It could be the postie or the newspaper person. Beware of strangers.
Lucky Number – 17
Lucky Colour – Ochre

Aries
21 Mar–20 Apr
If ever you're going to win something, it could be today. Don't miss a minute of it – days like this only happen once.
Lucky Numbers – 1, 2, 4, 6, 7, 8, 9, 14
Lucky Colour – Cerise

Taurus
21 Apr–21 May
The Moon in Saturn suggests you will be at peak physical fitness, so maybe you'll kick a goal, serve an ace or win a race.
Lucky Number – 1
Lucky Colour – Vermilion

Gemini
22 May–21 June
Today is ideal for making those important decisions, but if you find them too difficult to make, get someone else to make them.
Lucky Numbers – 4 or 9
Lucky Colour – Umber

Cancer
22 June–23July
You might come across the person of your dreams or a frog. But don't kiss the frog – all you'll end up with is a wart on the nose.
Lucky Number – 5
Lucky Colour – Scarlet

Leo
24 July–23 Aug
There is a chance you will go on a trip. It might be to the shops or over your two feet. Wherever it is, enjoy it.
Lucky Number – 3
Lucky Colour – Indigo

Virgo
24 Aug–23 Sept
Whatever you do, don't get out of bed today – you deserve a rest, but don't let the black cat on the bed.
Lucky Number – 13
Lucky Colour – Black

Libra
24 Sept–23 Oct
If you work hard you might get all your work right at school, or you might not. Whichever, work hard.
Lucky Number – 2
Lucky Colour – Sepia

Scorpio
24 Oct–22 Nov
There is a possibility you will be accident prone today so be careful undertaking activities such as bungy jumping and lion taming.
Lucky Number – 217
Luck Colour – Puce

Sagittarius
23 Nov–21 Dec
Money matters look promising. You might receive your pocket money, but don't let it burn a hole in your pocket! Ouch!
Lucky Number – 11
Lucky Colour – Carmine

Capricorn
22 Dec–20 Jan
Nothing. Not a thing will happen. Absolutely nothing! Why? Because Madame Guessalot can't think of any more predictions.
Lucky Number – 6
Lucky Colour – Turquoise

Text Type: Exposition – Horoscopes

Which star sign ...

1. ... suggests it would be a good day to buy a lottery ticket? ______________________
2. ... would you be if your birthday is on 14 May? ______________________
3. ... has a prediction suggesting romance? ______________________
4. ... has the largest lucky number? ______________________
5. ... warns you not to get involved in disputes? ______________________
6. ... is known as the goat? ______________________
7. ... has a prediction concerning finances? ______________________
8. ... suggests it might be an unlucky day? ______________________
9. Do any of the star signs make a definite prediction? If so, which one/s?

   ____

10. Many horoscopes are very vague and many people interpret them to fit their own situations. List three words from the Starscope that show that Madame Guessalot is unsure of her predictions. ______________ ______________ ______________
11. Magenta is a shade of red. Using a dictionary to help you, list three other shades of red that are given as Lucky Colours.

    ______________ ______________ ______________

12. List three shades of brown given as Lucky Colours.

    ______________ ______________ ______________

13. On the calendar, show the days of the year belonging to each star sign using the following colours. Capricorn (grey) has been done for you.

Capricorn (grey)	Aquarius (red)
Pisces (light blue)	Aries (orange)
Taurus (black)	Gemini (pink)
Cancer (light green)	Leo (yellow)
Virgo (dark blue)	Libra (brown)
Scorpio (dark green)	Sagittarius (purple)

JANUARY					
S		5	12	19	26
M		6	13	20	27
T		7	14	21	28
W	1	8	15	22	29
T	2	9	16	23	30
F	3	10	17	24	31
S	4	11	18	25	

FEBRUARY					
S		2	9	16	23
M		3	10	17	24
T		4	11	18	25
W		5	12	19	26
T		6	13	20	27
F		7	14	21	28
S	1	8	15	22	29

MARCH					
S	1	8	15	22	29
M	2	9	16	23	30
T	3	10	17	24	31
W	4	11	18	25	
T	5	12	19	26	
F	6	13	20	27	
S	7	14	21	28	

APRIL					
S		5	12	19	26
M		6	13	20	27
T		7	14	21	28
W	1	8	15	22	29
T	2	9	16	23	30
F	3	10	17	24	
S	4	11	18	25	

MAY					
S	31	3	10	17	24
M		4	11	18	25
T		5	12	19	26
W		6	13	20	27
T		7	14	21	28
F	1	8	15	22	29
S	2	9	16	23	30

JUNE					
S		7	14	21	28
M	1	8	15	22	29
T	2	9	16	23	30
W	3	10	17	24	
T	4	11	18	25	
F	5	12	19	26	
S	6	13	20	27	

JULY					
S		5	12	19	26
M		6	13	20	27
T		7	14	21	28
W	1	8	15	22	29
T	2	9	16	23	30
F	3	10	17	24	31
S	4	11	18	25	

AUGUST					
S	30	2	9	16	23
M	31	3	10	17	24
T		4	11	18	25
W		5	12	19	26
T		6	13	20	27
F		7	14	21	28
S	1	8	15	22	29

SEPTEMBER					
S		6	13	20	27
M		7	14	21	28
T	1	8	15	22	29
W	2	9	16	23	30
T	3	10	17	24	
F	4	11	18	25	
S	5	12	19	26	

OCTOBER					
S		4	11	18	25
M		5	12	19	26
T		6	13	20	27
W		7	14	21	28
T	1	8	15	22	29
F	2	9	16	23	30
S	3	10	17	24	31

NOVEMBER					
S	1	8	15	22	29
M	2	9	16	23	30
T	3	10	17	24	
W	4	11	18	25	
T	5	12	19	26	
F	6	13	20	27	
S	7	14	21	28	

DECEMBER					
S		6	13	20	27
M		7	14	21	28
T	1	8	15	22	29
W	2	9	16	23	30
T	3	10	17	24	31
F	4	11	18	25	
S	5	12	19	26	

Write a horoscope for yourself predicting things you would like to happen.

A Letter from the Goldfields

Ballarat Goldfields
17/5/1853

Dear Family,

I have been on the goldfields for five weeks now and things are not proceeding as well as I imagined. After purchasing my equipment, which was very expensive – 2 picks, 2 pans, 1 axe, 1 wedge, 2 buckets, a tent, plus my cooking utensils and a supply of food – I did not have enough money left to afford a coach. Luckily a group of miners offered me a lift in their wagon. I could not believe how many people were on the road to the goldfields, all filled with the same dream of 'striking it rich'. The weather was inclement on the trip up – it rained every day and it took several days to reach the goldfields.

The goldfields are very crowded and there are people from all parts of the world, including a very large Chinese population. The living conditions are very harsh. It gets very cold here, especially at night, and it has rained a lot. I think they should be called 'mudfields' instead of goldfields! I have only found a few specks of gold, and as food is scarce and very expensive, it certainly is not enough to live on. Not being a man of the land, I find digging all day extremely hard labour, and all for no reward. There are a lot of rough types on the goldfields; some are as tough as nails, and there are always arguments and fights among the miners, particularly after heavy bouts of drinking. A lot of miners (myself included) are very despondent about the miner's licence – £1 per month – and the constant inspections. One fellow, the other day, was dragged away by the troopers because he did not have his licence on his person – he had taken his shirt off and it was inside his pocket!

I think I am a fool to have sold up and gambled everything because of a fanciful dream. If I don't find gold soon I will have to abandon everything and make my way back to Melbourne.

Well, I live in hope. Trust this letter finds you all well.

Your loving son,
John

Text Type: Recount – Letter

Read John's letter and answer these questions.

1. What is the main message in the letter home? Tick the best alternative.
   - **a** Things are very expensive on the goldfields.
   - **b** There are a lot of Chinese people on the goldfields.
   - **c** Life on the goldfields is very difficult.
2. List three difficulties John experienced on the goldfields.

   ____

   ____

   ____
3. Why didn't John have enough money for the coach?

   ____
4. What does "striking it rich" mean?

   ____
5. What does John mean when he says, "not being a man of the land"?

   ____
6. John describes some of the miners as "tough as nails". This is a simile. Similes compare one thing with another. Write a different simile for:

   as tough as ____________

   Complete these similes.

   as old as __________ as cold as ___________ as hungry as ____________

   as black as _________ as flat as ___________ as keen as ______________
7. Give two reasons why the miners were displeased with the miner's licence.

   ____________________ ____________________
8. Find the words in the letter that mean:

   a buying ____________ **b** risked ____________ **c** regular __________

   d dear ____________ **e** severe ____________ **f** leave ____________

Moving on

Pretend that you are John's mother or father and write a short letter back to him.

Keeping an Eye on Things

Surveillance Report

Agent's Name: Kent Sharp **Date:** 16 October
Assisting Officer: Bronze Cuckoo
Weather Conditions: Sunny, 28 degrees
Subject: Operation Fadeout

8:00 a.m. Stationed ourselves in car dressed as telephone repair persons outside subject's house in Taylor Road.

8:10 a.m. Subject came out of house and walked three blocks to McDuck's Restaurant on corner of Albert Street. Agents followed in car.

8:20 a.m. Agent Cuckoo followed subject into restaurant and observed him ordering a Brekky-Burger, a serve of potato nuggets, a coffee thick shake and a chocolate doughnut. We both began to feel very hungry.

8:45 a.m. Subject emerged from restaurant licking his fingers. Got into car waiting for him in car park and drove away. Agent Sharp could not wait for Agent Cuckoo as she was still eating her double order of eggs and bacon.

9:05 a.m. Followed subject to train station where he was seen buying an interstate ticket. As he passed a tall woman in a red dress, he was seen to pass the ticket to her. She ate it. I was no longer hungry.

9:27 a.m. Subject bought a newspaper from the newsstand near the station entrance, opened it and took out a piece of paper. He then threw the newspaper away and put the piece of paper into his left sock.

9:32 a.m. Followed subject across road to movie theatre. He bought three tickets and went into the darkened theatre. I bought a ticket and followed him in. Found subject sprawled across three seats watching the movie. I sat just behind him. The film was really boring, a love story about this man and woman who were lost in the forest and … sorry, but I nodded off. When I woke up, I realised the subject had left the theatre.

10:50 a.m. Raced out of theatre to find subject standing on the footpath outside the theatre eating a huge bag of popcorn. I started to get really hungry again. I really think we agents should get a morning tea break. Subject walked back to station and got back into car. Nearly lost him as he had dropped a piece of popcorn and I was standing there drooling.

11:07 a.m. Jumped into car and followed subject along Main Street past three restaurants and billboards advertising chicken salads, giant ice-cream cones and other yummy things. Started to chew my sleeve at this stage.

11:35 a.m. Followed subject to airport. Went into terminal where subject took piece of paper from sock and made a phone call from a booth. Overheard only a few words: "fish", "sushi" and "sausages". Took off my shoe and started chewing the leather.

11:48 a.m. Subject finished telephone conversation and walked to Mr Han's Chinese Restaurant where he ordered steak and black bean sauce with boiled noodles, a serve of special fried rice and six dim sims followed by banana fritters and ice-cream. Luckily I found a few dried grains of rice on my table that I was able to gulp down.

12:42 p.m. Subject left restaurant. I followed, chewing my tie. Subject got into car and drove back to city.

12:56 p.m. Subject pulled up at police headquarters. Police at door saluted him. I asked who he was. I was told he was the head undercover man.
And I had missed my lunch … again!

- **Text Type:** Information – Report

Here are the answers. Now you have to write the questions.

1 Q: ____________________________________

A: He put it in his left sock.

2 Q: ____________________________________

A: Mr Han's

3 Q: ____________________________________

A: Three blocks from his house

4 Q: ____________________________________

A: In the car park

5 Q: ____________________________________

A: To a tall woman in a red dress

6 Q: ____________________________________

A: So he could lie across three seats while he was watching the movie

7 Q: ____________________________________

A: He chewed the leather.

8 Q: ____________________________________

A: When he woke up

9 Q: ____________________________________

A: Because Agent Cuckoo was still eating her eggs and bacon

10 Q: ____________________________________

A: From a newsstand near the station entrance.

Moving on

Draw up a comic strip to show what happened while the agent was following the subject.

Week 32

A Bright Spark

Combine a bit of knowledge with electric circuits to make a Knowledge Board.

You will need:

- a piece of card approximately 20 centimetres square
- 8 paper fasteners
- 7 pieces of electrical wire – bare the ends
- a battery
- a bulb and bulb holder
- a pair of scissors
- sticky tape
- a pen

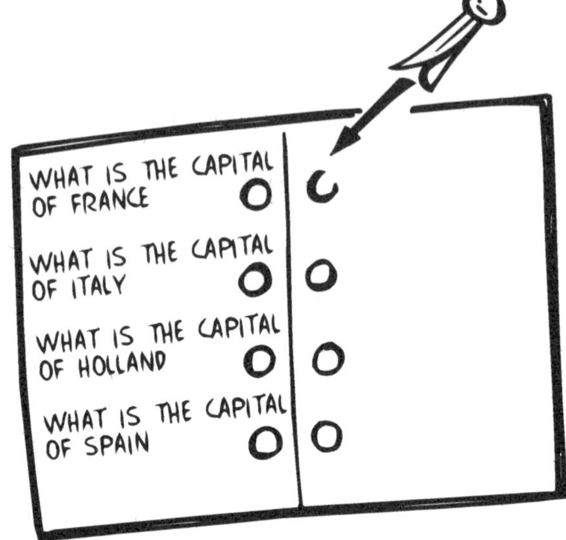

Instuctions:

1 Write down four questions on any subject on the left-hand side of the card. On the right-hand side write the answers, but next to the wrong questions.

2 Push a paper fastener through the card next to each question and answer.

3 On the other side of the card use four of the wires to connect up each question with the correct answer by wrapping wire around the paper fasteners.

4 Connect a wire between the battery and the bulb holder. Then connect another wire to the battery and the final wire to the bulb holder.

5 Get a classmate to touch one wire to a paper fastener next to a question and the other wire to the paper fastener of the answer they think is the correct one. If correct, a circuit will be formed and the bulb will light up.

WARNING Batteries are safe to use, but never experiment with mains electricity. Death by electrocution can result.

Text Type: Procedural – Experiment / Instructions

Are you a bright spark? Answer these questions to find out.

1. How many pieces of equipment do you need to make a Knowledge Board?
   ____
2. On which side of the card do you write the questions? ______________________________
3. How do you connect the wires to the paper fasteners?
   ____
4. How many wires are connected to the
   a bulb holder? ______________ **b** battery? ______________
5. After placing one wire on a question, why does the bulb light up if the other wire is placed on the correct answer?
   ____
6. What happens if you connect a question to the wrong answer? ______________
   Why? ______________________________
7. Write down the four questions and answers (see step **1**) as if you were making a Knowledge Board. Swap with a friend and match up the questions and answers by ruling lines.
   ______________________ • • ______________
   ______________________ • • ______________
   ______________________ • • ______________
   ______________________ • • ______________
8. You must NEVER place the wires connected to the bulb holder into a power point. Why not?
   ____
9. Connect the correct answers to the questions on this Knowledge Board.

AUSTRALIA'S CAPITAL CITIES

New South Wales	❍	❍	Adelaide
Tasmania	❍	❍	Perth
Victoria	❍	❍	Hobart
Queensland	❍	❍	Sydney
Western Australia	❍	❍	Darwin
South Australia	❍	❍	Melbourne
Northern Territory	❍	❍	Brisbane

Moving on

Get a battery, a bulb holder and a bulb, some wire and the other necessary pieces of equipment and make your own Knowledge Board.

Week 33

Rhyming Time

A feature of the Australian language is the way some words are put into rhyming slang. For example, a road can be called a *frog and toad*.

The following story is written partly in rhyming slang. Try saying the words normally used to help you work out the meanings.

I was crossing the ***frog and toad*** when a huge truck caught my ***meat pie***. It was travelling so fast that I had to get my ***billy lids*** to wait before crossing at the ***Johnny Horner***. The driver was out of ***Friar Tuck*** because a policeman pulled a whistle out of his ***sky rocket*** and blew it to attract the attention of his ***garden gates*** in a nearby police car.

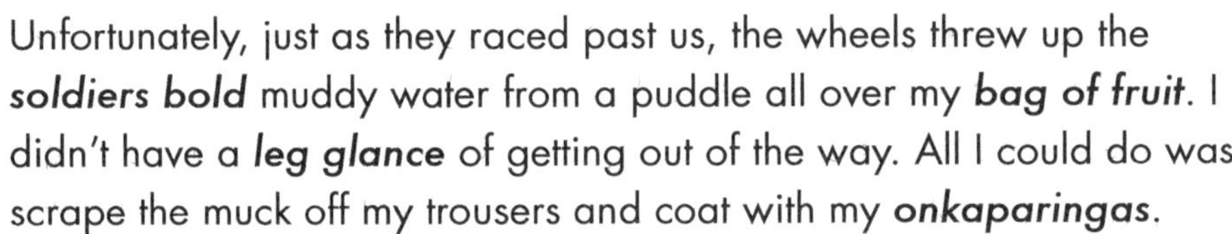

Unfortunately, just as they raced past us, the wheels threw up the ***soldiers bold*** muddy water from a puddle all over my ***bag of fruit***. I didn't have a ***leg glance*** of getting out of the way. All I could do was scrape the muck off my trousers and coat with my ***onkaparingas***.

I wiped my ***plates of meat*** on the kerb and took the children by the ***Warwick Farms*** to have a ***Captain Cook*** at what had happened. Their little ***jam tarts*** were beating really fast with the shock. By now the police and the truck had almost reached the other side of ***night gown***. All I could think of now was that I was hungry for a ***Nelly Bly*** with plenty of ***dead horse***.

Just then I was amazed to see a ***tea leaf*** dash from a ***tomfoolery*** shop carrying gold and silver bracelets in both his ***German bands***. Thinking quickly, I stuck out my ***Mallee root*** and tripped him up. He fell flat on his ***boat race***. You might not believe this story, but I can tell you that I never tell ***pork pies***.

A Rhyming Slang Dictionary

Use the words that appear in the story as the start to your own rhyming slang dictionary.

1. bag of fruit ______________________
2. billy lids ______________________
3. boat race ______________________
4. Captain Cook ______________________
5. dead horse ______________________
6. Friar Tuck ______________________
7. frog and toad ______________________
8. garden gates ______________________
9. jam tarts ______________________
10. Johnny Horner ______________________
11. leg glance ______________________
12. Mallee root ______________________
13. meat pie ______________________
14. Nelly Bly ______________________
15. night gown ______________________
16. onkaparingas ______________________
17. plates of meat ______________________
18. pork pies ______________________
19. sky rocket ______________________
20. soldiers bold ______________________
21. tea leaf ______________________
22. tomfoolery ______________________
23. Warwick Farms ______________________

Moving on

1 You can make up some rhyming slang of your own for words you commonly use.

Examples: *school* could be *golden rule*
tennis could be *Dennis the Menace*

2 Draw pictures to illustrate some of your rhyming slang words.

Is He a Champion?

THE SPORTING STAR • • • Wednesday 11 Sept. 1929

Is He a Champion?

The towering and powerful-looking 'Big Red' may just prove to be a world-class racehorse.

Yes, Phar Lap is proving that he CAN win races and is beginning to repay the confidence shown by trainer Harry Telford. After his first place in the Rosehill Guineas, Phar Lap followed up with a brilliant win in the AJC Derby last Saturday, setting a world record time.

Now the big chestnut is poised to possibly dominate this year's racing calendar. Jockey Jim Pike hinted at his potential after his 2nd in the Chelmsford Stakes, prior to the running of the Rosehill Guineas. "I couldn't hold him back! It was like trying to slow down an express train."

Things weren't always so rosy for trainer Telford. After purchasing the horse, unseen, from New Zealand for 160 guineas for owner Dave Davis, Telford found himself fronted with a scrawny looking horse whose face was covered in warts and boils. Davis is reported to have commented, "It looks like a cross between a kangaroo and a sheepdog. Sell him Harry." But Telford held a belief that Phar Lap's breeding – by Nightraid (sire) out of Entreaty (dam) – would produce a champion. On both sides he is related to Carbine, the legendary 1890 Melbourne Cup winner.

At his first start, Phar Lap finished last and his next three races were no better. He broke this drought, winning a maiden handicap in April this year, but his next four races as a 3-year-old were less than encouraging. But all this changed dramatically at his next outing, the Chelmsford Stakes.

Telford has set the horse very rigorous training schedules – running him up and down sand hills, and the once gangling eyesore is now a 17-hand powerhouse. Asked during the week where he got the name Phar Lap, Telford explained that following sarcastic taunts of 'Lightning' by other trainers, an Asian student was asked for a translation. The student wrote down 'Farlap'. Telford wanted a seven-letter name as the past four Melbourne Cup winners had seven letters in their names. The student simply crossed out the 'F' and replaced it with 'Ph'. Hence the name Phar Lap.

A Melbourne Cup! Is this horse, now being dubbed in some circles 'The Red Terror', capable of winning a Melbourne Cup? Telford seems to think so. And I, for one, agree.

What have you learnt about Phar Lap?

1. How did Phar Lap perform in his first race?

   ____

2. Who was Phar Lap's mother? ______________ father? ______________

3. How many races did Phar Lap win before setting a world record for the AJC Derby?

   ____

4. What did jockey Jim Pike compare Phar Lap to after his 2nd in the Chelmsford Stakes?

   ____

5. Phar Lap was nicknamed 'Big Red'. What other two nicknames was he given in the article?

   ______________ ______________

6. When other trainers called Phar Lap 'Lightning', do you think they thought he was as fast as lightning? Why / Why not?

   ____

   ____

7. Why did trainer Harry Telford want a seven-letter name for the horse?

   ____

8. Why did Telford believe that Phar Lap would be a champion?

   ____

   ____

9. What does the writer of this article predict for Phar Lap?

   ____

10. Write a brief caption for the photo using some of the information from the article.

    ____

    ____

Moving on

Do some research to find the answers to these questions: How many races did Phar Lap have in his career? How many did he win? What was his total prize money? What, when and where was his last race?

Spidery Facts: Did You Know ...?

Some books say that there are over 20 000 species of spiders, while others put this figure at over 40 000, with the smallest spiders being the size of a pin head. The tarantulas that are found in South America can be as big as dinner plates. However, the largest spider is the Goliath Bird-eating Spider. One captured male had a leg span of 28 centimetres.

Spiders have two main body parts – a joined head and chest known as the cephalothorax and the rear part, which contains the spinnerets, called the abdomen. Each of the eight legs has six joints.

Almost all spiders have more than two eyes, with most having two rows of four eyes. Despite all these eyes, they do not have good eyesight and use their legs and pedipalps to feel their way around.

A fear of spiders is called arachnophobia. A film by this name about a giant spider terrified cinema audiences. Spiders belong to the group called arachnids and are also called arthropods, which means they are invertebrates that have jointed legs and segmented bodies.

Spiders have been used as 'guard dogs'. A gallery owner in Jarrow, England, hired two South American tarantulas from a pet shop to guard a jewellery display. At $10 a month it was a lot cheaper than the $9000 to hire human guards.

The Daddy-long-legs is said to be the most venomous spider but it can't inject its venom. The most venomous spider in the world is the Brazilian Wandering Spider.

Spiders don't have bones. Their insides are protected by a hard layer of skin called a cuticle. This external skeleton is known as an exoskeleton. As spiders grow they shed their skin and stay hidden until their new skin hardens.

Spiders produce silk from glands in the abdomen known as spinnerets. The silk starts as a sticky liquid that hardens when exposed to air and forms very light but very strong thread. Spiders have oil on their legs to stop them from sticking to their own silk.

Spiders cannot eat solid food. They kill their prey by injecting venom through their fangs. The prey is then covered in strong digestive juices so that a spider's digestion actually begins outside the body. The juices turn the edible parts of the prey into liquid food, and muscles in the spider's stomach are used to suck the food into the digestive tract.

In most cases the female spider is bigger than the male of the species and lives much longer. (Female tarantulas have been known to live for more than 25 years.) The Black Widow gets its name because the female often kills and eats the male after mating.

Other Spider Facts

- Some spiders feed their spiderlings.
- Spinning of a web is usually done at night.
- Spiders pretend to be dead when they are frightened.
- Spiders lay their eggs in a silk cocoon.
- The Wolf Spider does not have a home and carries its egg sac around on its back.
- Spiders can grow new legs if any are lost.

Text Type: Information – Factual Description

What have you learnt about spiders?

1. If the leg joints on a spider are called knees, how many knees does a spider have? ________
2. How many eyes do most spiders have? ________________
3. What is an exoskeleton? ____
4. Why don't spiders stick to the webs they build?

   ____

5. What is unusual about the spider's digestive system?

   ____

6. What tells you that non-fiction books can vary on the information they provide?

   ____

   ____

7. Why do you think tarantulas would make such good 'guard dogs'?

   ____

8. What is the fear of spiders called? ____________________________

   Phobia, which means 'fear of', comes from the Greek word ***phobos***, meaning 'fear'. Use a dictionary to find out what kinds of fears people suffer from when they have:

   a claustrophobia ____________________ **b** hydrophobia ____________________

   c acrophobia ____________________ **d** microphobia ____________________

   e zoophobia ____________________ **f** phobophobia ____________________

9. Use the words in the box to label the spider.

abdomen	fang	pedipalps
spinnerets	eyes	leg
cephalothorax		

10. What else would you like to know about spiders? Write one more question about spiders that you would like to know the answer to.

    ____

    ____

Moving on

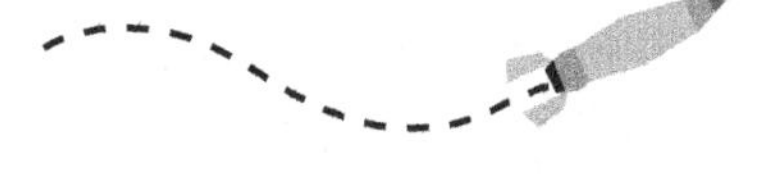

Do some research to find the answer to the question you wrote.

Comprehension Focus: Literal Questioning / Labelling a Diagram

Psst

Have you heard that

____

has surely and
successfully
completed a
sensational
_________ weeks of

Comprehension Once a Week
Book 6

Signed: ________________

Date: ________________